CREATIVE THERAPY II:
52 MORE
EXERCISES
FOR GROUPS

Jane Dossick & Eugene Shea

Illustrated by Eugene Shea

Professional Resource Exchange, Inc.
Sarasota, Florida

This book was produced in the USA using a patented European binding technology called Otabind. We chose this unique binding because it allows pages to lay flat for photocopying, is stronger than standard bindings for this purpose, and has numerous advantages over spiral-binding (e.g., less chance of damage in shipping, no unsightly spiral marks on photocopies, and a spine you can read when the book is on your bookshelf).

Printed in the United States of America

ISBN: 0-943158-60-5
Library of Congress Catalog Card Number: 88-42577

The copy editor for this book was Judy Warinner, the production supervisor was Debbie Fink, the graphics coordinator was Laurie Girsch, and the cover designer was Bill Tabler.

For Joanne, Philip, and Stephen

TABLE OF CONTENTS

INTRODUCTION

WHO SHOULD USE THIS BOOK?

Like its predecessor, *Creative Therapy: 52 Exercises for Groups*, this book has been designed as a practical guide to assist psychotherapists, group leaders, and specially trained teachers in mental health facilities, nursing homes, day programs, inpatient psychiatric units, special education programs, and support groups. It may be used as an adjunct to the psychotherapeutic treatment of such varied problems as Alzheimer's disease, schizophrenia, mental retardation, and depression.

The huge success of *Creative Therapy: 52 Exercises for Groups*, led to the development of this sequel, which contains 52 *new* therapeutic exercises complete with illustrations that may be photocopied for group members. The exercises serve as an avenue to therapeutic discussions of important issues that might not be shared through other techniques. Additionally, we have received feedback regarding the use of these exercises with the individual treatment of children. We have learned that children may enjoy the exercises, and are consequently less inhibited about sharing fears, concerns, and fantasies.

As we did in the previous work, this new book explains methods of energizing a group, and takes both new and experienced group leaders through the stages for effective implementation of structured exercises. We have used these kinds of materials successfully in a major New York City long-term care hospital. We find that these exercises can help group members develop interactive skills, motivate less verbal individuals to contribute to group discussions, and encourage group cohesiveness.

WHAT IS IN THIS BOOK?

Creative Therapy II: 52 More Exercises for Groups is presented in an uncomplicated fashion so that the exercises will be nonthreatening to group members. The format allows the leader to refer to directions for each group meeting, and to photocopy the accompanying illustration, which becomes each member's worksheet. In each exercise, members complete a picture that focuses on a particular theme. A discussion follows in which the members discuss what their completed pictures reveal about themselves. Each member is able to look at his or her own illustration and express an initial response that might otherwise have been forgotten. The illustrations are intentionally simple to encourage participants to express themselves as freely as possible.

HOW DO YOU USE THIS BOOK?

Creative Therapy II: 52 More Exercises for Groups combines the structured expression of art groups with the therapeutic communication of verbal discussion groups. The worksheet provided with each exercise serves as a springboard to discussion for group members. Each exercise is accompanied by a step-by-step set of instructions for the group leader.

Creative Therapy II: 52 More Exercises for Groups

Group members sit at a table, preferably in a circle. The leader hands out photocopies of the chosen exercise to members at the beginning of the session. The leader should seek to involve members immediately by asking about the picture.

The group leader introduces the theme, describes the exercise according to the instructions that accompany each drawing, and asks for feedback and comments from the group members. This initial discussion should be used to prepare the members for the task that follows.

Next, group members are given a time frame and directed to "fill in" or complete the exercise with their responses. Additional supplies such as crayons, markers, or pencils may be handed out at this time.

It is important to be certain that everyone has a clear understanding of the task. If questions arise, it is recommended that members be encouraged to ask each other to paraphrase the instructions. In this way members become actively involved and discover they can be helpful to one another.

Setting up a time frame is an important aspect of the structured exercise. These projects work best if the group members understand how much time is set aside for drawing, and how much time is for discussion. For example, in a 1-hour group, 20 minutes might be used for explanation and drawing, and 40 minutes for discussion.

These exercises should be nonthreatening. To reduce anxiety, group leaders should explain that content is more important than artistic talent, and that the drawings are used simply to promote discussion. Some members may be resistant to drawing because of self-consciousness or physical limitations. Encouragement is helpful, but too much encouragement may become stressful. An alternative is to avoid adding extra pressure by allowing anxious members to write rather than draw their interpretations.

Group discussion immediately follows the drawing period. The leader should state a few minutes ahead of time when this will take place. Once group discussion begins, all members' comments should then be directed to the group as a whole.

Members are asked to volunteer to discuss their interpretations. The leader becomes a catalyst to promote and encourage verbal interaction and help focus the discussion. As members see one another present and receive feedback, more may volunteer to discuss their work.

WHAT ARE THE BENEFITS?

Projective art tasks introduce ideas that provide encouragement to groups searching for a common theme (Dalley, 1984). In addition, these structured exercises have a variety of other uses: to initiate members into a group process; as a warm-up technique; to help a group work through a particular stage in its development; to enhance group members' abilities to interact and share freely; to focus on a specific group need; and to help reduce group members' anxiety and uncertainty. For example, if used with children, the exercises allow the child to indirectly or directly express important ideas, fantasies, and feelings. Significant information about family members and dynamics are often shared as a result of this approach. It must be understood, however, that these techniques are intended as a tool - as one part of a total approach to meet the goals of a particular group.

Structured exercises are a way of accelerating group interaction. Getting in touch with suppressed emotions helps the group as a whole as well as the individual members. Specific exercises may be chosen to help the group work through a particular problem (Hansen, Warner, & Smith, 1980).

Yalom (1983) describes the use of structured exercises with lower-level, inpatient psychotherapy groups. These groups often consist of members with a limited attention span, fearfulness, and confusion. Structured exercises may help such members express themselves. The use of art or drawing exercises is especially helpful in fostering self-expression. These exercises may also stimulate group interest and provide variety. We believe the exercises in *Creative Therapy II: 52 More Exercises for Groups* are very effective with this type of group.

Structured exercises also help insure that no one dominates, and that everyone has an opportunity to speak. A balance of verbal input is created. Monopolistic members must develop self-control to allow other members to have their turns. Shy or nonverbal members profit from the required participation, such as described by Levin and Kurtz (1974). These authors studied the effects of structured exercises in human relations groups and concluded that the inactive person benefits from a change in behavioral expectations. Greater opportunity for participation generates more ego-involvement, self-perceived personality changes, and increased group unity.

How does group therapy help group members? Feedback from one's peers, if properly channeled, can be a potent therapeutic force, promoting qualitative changes in self-expression, growth toward self-actualization, and changes in interpersonal behavior.

In his classic work on group psychotherapy, Yalom identifies key curative factors associated with the group process. We believe that many of the exercises included in *Creative Therapy II: 52 More Exercises for Groups* facilitate the curative process. Generally, the exercises encourage sharing and development of trust among group members. The drawings illustrate common fears and anxieties and allow group members to see how each share many of the same concerns. Through the use of the illustrations, members are encouraged to support each other in finding solutions to problems and to learn to support each others' needs. Skilled therapists will strategically use the exercises to support the development of other curative factors within the group.

WHAT ARE THE LIMITATIONS
OF THESE EXERCISES?

Through experience, we have found these exercises and materials to be of great value. It is important, however, to realize the limitations of their use. As we have said, these exercises are to be used as a springboard to discussion as an adjunct to other therapies.

Yalom (1985) describes possible negative effects structured exercises can have on groups. He suggests, for example, that they can create an atmosphere where critical stages of group interaction may be passed over. Structured exercises may also plunge the group members into sharing significant negative and positive feelings too quickly. In addition, the group leader may be too heavily relied upon by the members. This dissipates a group's' potential effectiveness as a therapeutic agent.

The Lieberman, Yalom, and Miles encounter group project (1973) studied how structured exercises influence groups. The leaders who used relatively large numbers of structured exercises with their groups were often more popular with group members. However, group members were found to have a significantly lower outcome level than members participating in groups using fewer structured exercises.

There must be a balance to the use of structured exercises. The degree to which they should be used must be carefully weighed by the group leader; otherwise the leader runs the risk of reducing the group's potential and infantilizing the members. Some factors that determine the amount and type of structuring to be employed are the type of group, member characteristics, and the leaders' theoretical orientation (M. S. Corey & G. Corey, 1987).

Additionally, the group leader should keep in mind three of the considerations noted by Pfeiffer and Jones (1983). First, structured exercises should address the specific goals and purposes of the group. The leader should choose exercises directed at interests, concerns, or problems of individual members or of the group as a whole. Second, a more than casual understanding of the members is important, because revelation and exploration of fantasy can be threatening and anxiety-provoking. Less threatening exercises are recommended for groups with anxious or guarded members to promote openness rather than defensiveness. Third, different issues surface at various stages of group development. Groups will function best when the level of feedback expected corresponds to the developmental stage of the group. In early stages of group development, exercises that focus on openness and building trust are more appropriate. Exercises that focus on critical feedback and appraisal will be more successful in the later stages of group development.

CONCLUSION

Creative Therapy II: 52 More Exercises for Groups should offer rewarding experiences for both group leaders and group members. The structured exercises in this book make it easier for group members to focus ideas, feelings, and experiences related to the topic of discussion. Members further benefit from revealing themselves, exchanging feedback, and supporting one another emotionally.

The purpose of this book, however, is first and foremost to help group leaders, therapists, and teachers conduct their groups by providing a framework for successful group experiences. Through the use of specific suggestions, we describe the procedures necessary for group leaders to handle the widest variety of group therapy applications.

In addition, the use of these exercises may also help to alert group leaders to issues for further exploration in individual counseling or other group therapies. Although designed primarily for groups, with slight modification these exercises can be used in individual treatment. In particular, they may be most helpful for children.

REFERENCES

Corey, M. S., & Corey, G. (1987). *Groups: Process & Practice* (3rd ed.). Monterey, CA: Brooks/Cole.

Dalley, T. (1984). *Art As Therapy: An Introduction to the Use of Art As a Therapeutic Technique.* New York: Tavistock.

Hansen, J. C., Warner, R. W., & Smith, E. J. (1980). *Group Counseling: Theory and Process* (2nd ed.). Chicago: Rand McNally.

Levin, E. N., & Kurtz, R. R. (1974). Structured and non structured human relations training. *Journal of Counseling Psychology, 21,* 526-531.

Lieberman, M. A., Yalom, I. D., & Miles, M. B. (1973). *Encounter Groups: First Facts.* New York: Basic Books.

Pfeiffer, J. W., & Jones, J. E. (1983). *A Handbook of Structured Experiences for Human Relations Training: Reference Guide to Handbooks and Annuals.* San Diego: University Associates.

Shulman, L. (1979). *The Skills of Helping Individuals and Groups.* Itasca, IL: F. E. Peacock.

Yalom, I. D. (1983). *Inpatient Group Psychotherapy.* New York: Basic Books.

Yalom, I. D. (1985). *The Theory and Practice of Group Psychotherapy* (3rd ed.). New York: Basic Books.

CREATIVE THERAPY II: 52 MORE EXERCISES FOR GROUPS

Exercise 1

THE TALK SHOW

Purpose:

1. To promote group identity and cohesion.
2. To provide an opportunity for open communication and the expression of negative feelings.
3. To encourage empathy and support.

Materials:

One photocopy of the illustration for each group member; crayons, markers, pens, or pencils.

Description:

A. The group leader hands out the materials.
B. The leader begins a discussion of the various types of forums and formats for expressing opinions, exchanging information, and sharing experiences with others.
C. Members are asked to imagine being a talk-show host.
D. They are guided to focus on the empty couch in the illustration and imagine it as part of the set of a talk show. Members are encouraged to think about provocative guests that would offer topics of interest and also interact with the audience.

Group Discussion:

Members share their illustrations and reveal what they imagine each guest is talking about. Other members are encouraged to act as the talk-show audience, and to ask follow-up questions of each guest. The group members may even want to debate some of the controversial issues introduced by the guests on the talk show.

This exercise is effective with a variety of group types at any stage of development. It can be interpreted on many levels, and may help members express personal concerns in an accepting environment.

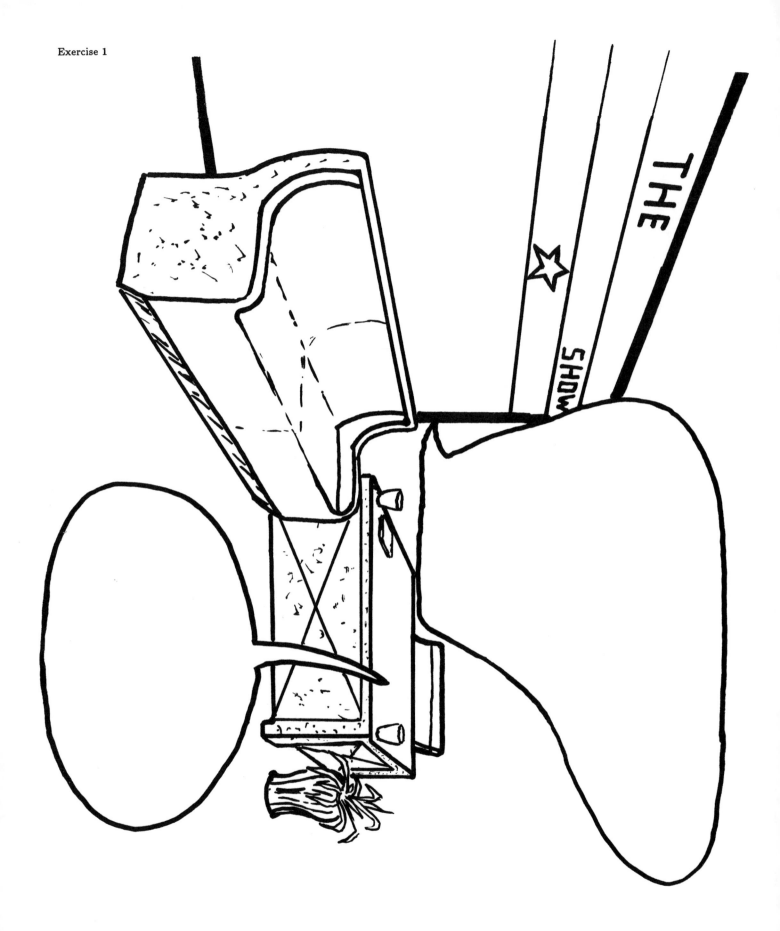

Exercise 2

THE STATE LOTTERY

Purpose:

1. To express individual needs through fantasy.
2. To provide an opportunity for sharing feelings about what might be missing from each other's lives.
3. To promote group interaction in a nonthreatening way.

Materials:

One photocopy for each member; pens, pencils, markers, or crayons.

Description:

A. The significance that numbers such as birth dates have in people's lives is explored with group members.
B. The materials are distributed.
C. Within the illustration, members draw what they would do with their winnings if they actually won the lottery.
D. In the space provided, members are asked to fill in those numbers that have special meaning to them.

Group Discussion:

Members take turns describing how the imagined lottery winnings would be spent. Members tell how this windfall could change their lives. The leader helps members explore similarities and differences in choices. Members exchange views on what these choices might reveal about each other. Members then share the significance (if any) that their "winning" numbers have played in their lives.

This exercise may help leaders recognize some unfulfilled needs of members. It is effective with any group type, in all stages of development, and may be an effective tool for groups in the early stages of development to help become better acquainted with one another.

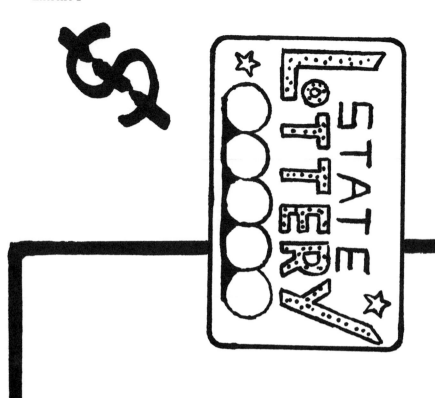

Exercise 3

LEFT OUT OF THE CROWD

Purpose:

1. To recognize feelings of rejection.
2. To give and receive advice in order to better understand life experiences.
3. To promote empathy and support.

Materials:

One photocopy of the illustration for each member; pens, pencils, crayons, or markers.

Description:

A. The leader initiates a discussion about the social and psychological aspects of "feeling left out of the crowd."
B. The materials are distributed and the leader asks members to think about a situation in which he or she has felt this way.
C. Members are told to first draw the situation they were excluded from in the lower right box labeled ". . . The Crowd."
D. Next, they draw how it felt and what they did about it in the upper left box labeled "Left Out . . . ."

Group Discussion:

Members each describe the particular situation that they felt left out of. The group is encouraged to explore this subject, as well as provide empathy and support. Members focus on what the individual did about being left out, and explore the alternative choices they might have made in that situation. Though actual situations (and how they were dealt with) may vary, the leader should help members concentrate on feelings shared in common.

This exercise is recommended for groups in which members are more acquainted with one another, as they need to feel secure in order to reveal uncomfortable experiences and feelings of rejection. It is effective with all group types as it may be interpreted on many levels.

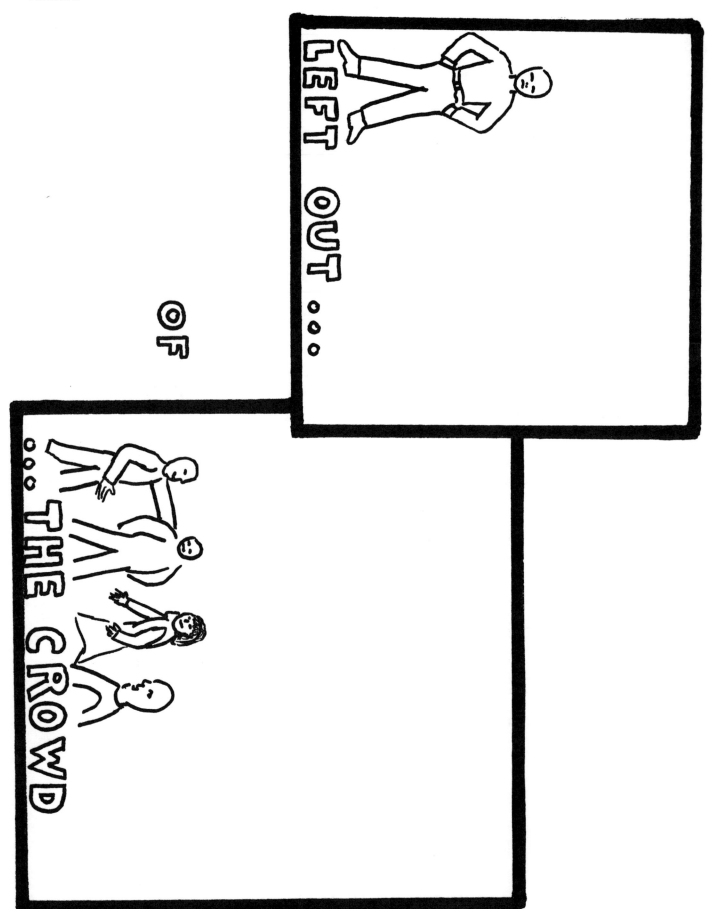

Exercise 4

THE FAMILY FIGHT

Purpose:

1. To develop insight into interpersonal relationships.
2. To reinforce trust through self-disclosure.

Materials:

One photocopy of the illustration for each member; pens or pencils.

Description:

A. While handing out materials, the group leader asks members to talk about how family fights are often emotionally charged, no matter what the argument is about.
B. The group looks at the frame on the bottom left of the illustration, and discusses the tension and emotion involved.
C. In response to the question "Who started it and why," members are asked to individually make up a story that might have led to the family fight. The story begins in the word bubble, and, if necessary, continues on the back of the page.

Group Discussion:

Each member reads their story of how the fight started, and describes related emotions. Then, they tell if the picture reminded them of any situation that influenced their response. After all captions are read, members are asked to reveal whose cartoon most closely resembled their own family.

Because the projective aspect of this exercise is less subtle, it is recommended for groups in which members are more acquainted with one another. It is effective with a wide range of group types, because arguments over either abstract or concrete issues reveal a great deal about interpersonal dynamics.

Exercise 5

THE SWIMMING POOL

Purpose:

  1. To share memories and compare experiences.
  2. To promote insight into individual behavior.
  3. To explore feelings of self-evaluation.

Materials:

One photocopy of the illustration for each member; pencils, crayons, or markers.

Description:

  A. The leader shows the illustration to the group and describes the swimming pool as representative of a big event that took place in their lives. The leader makes certain that members understand (a) the "dive" as meeting a challenge head on, (b) the "slide" as quickly entering a situation but feeling little control, and (c) the "steps" as proceeding slowly and cautiously.
  B. While handing out the materials, the leader tells members to recall a major event in their lives and think about whether they dove, slid, or gradually stepped into it.
  C. The group is told to draw the event in the pool and draw themselves on the diving board, slide, or steps according to how they think they approached the situation.

Group Discussion:

Each member shares the event depicted in the swimming pool. They describe the feelings they had that related to either diving, sliding, or stepping into the illustrated situation. Other members are encouraged to tell if they would have approached this big event the same way.

This exercise is most effective with groups that are able to think abstractly, in all stages of development.

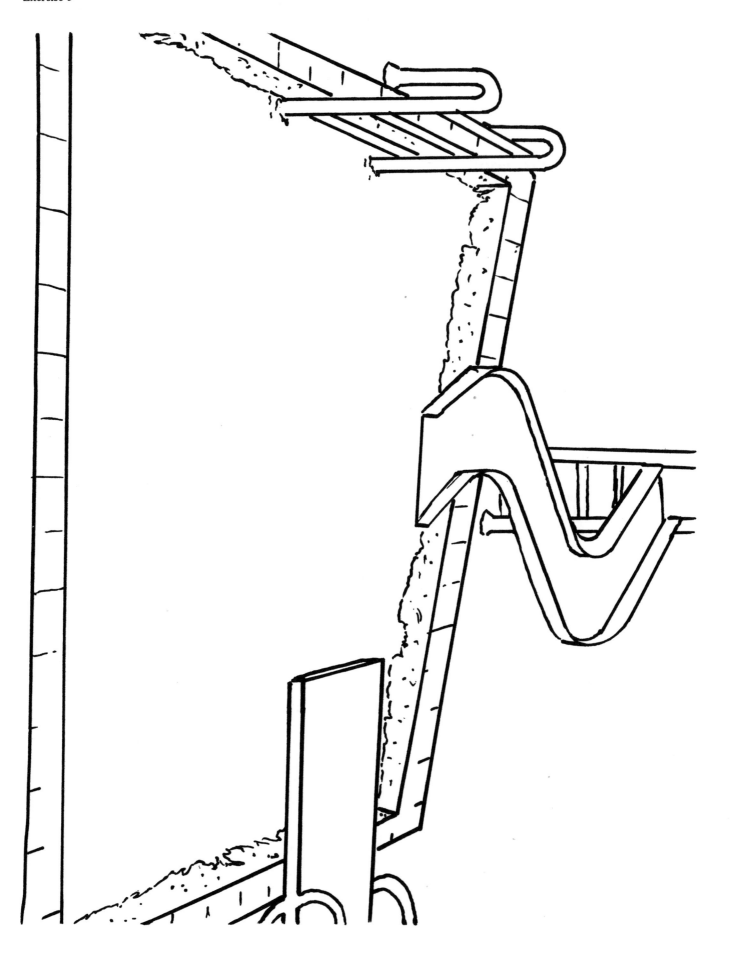

Exercise 6

THE ROAD NOT TAKEN

Purpose:

1. To incorporate group feedback into self-evaluation.
2. To promote empathy.
3. To develop group cohesion through mutual self-disclosure.

Materials:

One photocopy of the illustration for each member; crayons, markers, pens, or pencils.

Description:

A. The materials are distributed, and the leader asks how the illustrated road relates to life choices group members have made in various times in their lives.
B. Members recall life choices made that they now have come to regret.
C. They illustrate these on the depicted road where the sign reads "Road Taken." They draw in the choice that in retrospect they should have made on the road with the sign "Road Not Taken." They include what the outcome of this choice might have been.

Group Discussion:

Each member describes his or her illustration. First the member tells why he or she feels the wrong choice was made. The member then describes what the other road could have led to. The group leader encourages others to understand why the member initially chose the road and the circumstances which led to it. Frequently, group members are empathetic and supportive when regretted life choices are revealed.

Group members need to be able to think abstractly to complete this exercise. It is most effective when used in groups in the later stages of development.

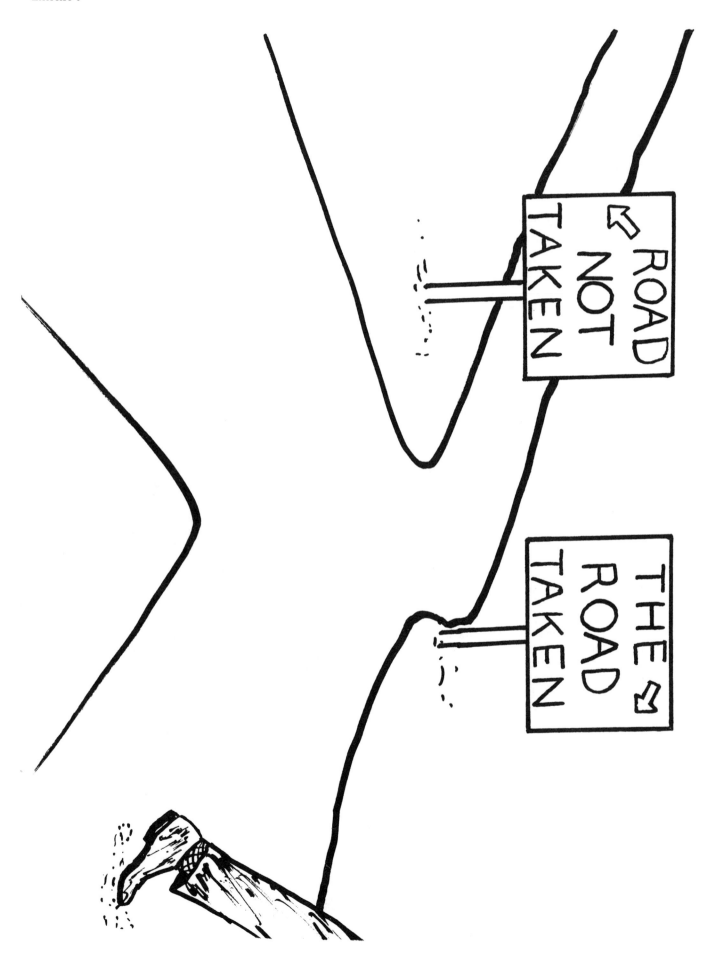

Exercise 7

MOVING AWAY

Purpose:

1. To share feelings and fears about adjusting to change.
2. To empathize with one another about feelings of separation.

Materials:

One photocopy of the illustration for each member; crayons, markers, pens, or pencils.

Description:

A. The leader shares the illustration with the group, and asks members to imagine moving away from where they live at present.
B. While handing out the materials, the group members are asked to think about the positive and negative aspects of where they live now. They are told to consider the things they like and dislike about their neighborhood, neighbors, and their living conditions.
C. In the window, members illustrate who and what they would miss if they moved away.

Group Discussion:

Members describe their illustrations and the leader asks them to share their feelings about moving away from familiar people, situations, and surroundings. The group members are encouraged to share what they think these feelings reveal about each other. Similarities which evolve around moving away from negative situations and people will emerge.

This exercise is effective with all group types in all stages of development. It is a useful tool to introduce new members to one another in the early stages. It is also effective in later stages of development where members may want to clarify feelings about possible group termination, or actual fears about leaving the place they reside in.

Exercise 8

THE SCRAPBOOK

Purpose:

1. To share memories and compare experiences.
2. To promote group identity and cohesion.
3. To understand group dynamics.

Materials:

One photocopy of the illustration for each member; pens, pencils, crayons, or markers.

Description:

A. The leader initiates a discussion of how memories of experiences and relationships influence how we feel now.
B. The materials are handed out. The leader asks members to think of any experiences, events or interpersonal relationships that have taken place within their group that have had an impact on them. Group members are reminded that these can be negative or positive.
C. Members are asked to illustrate these memories either as a picture in the box or in words, or both.

Group Discussion:

Each member describes his or her scrapbook to the group, and reveals what effect these recollections have had personally. The leader encourages questions about these feelings and notes similarities and differences in choices of illustrations in each scrapbook.

When memories about past conflict or discord within the group are shared, members are encouraged to be supportive of one another. A frequent outcome is that members may reminisce about people who are no longer part of the group.

If negative experiences surface during this exercise, they may provide an opportunity to focus on unresolved issues within the group.

This exercise is effective with well-integrated groups in the later stages of group development.

REMEMBER WHEN WE

Exercise 9

AT THE TRADING POST

Purpose:

1. To promote feedback about self-evaluation.
2. To increase understanding and acceptance among members.
3. To compare viewpoints and perspectives about self-evaluation.

Materials:

One photocopy of the illustration for each member; crayons, pens, pencils, or markers.

Description:

A. The leader begins the exercise by introducing the idea that our personalities are made up of strengths and weaknesses. The group explores the concept of being able to trade personalities.
B. While handing out materials, the leader tells group members to think about their own personalities and those aspects of themselves they would like to change.
C. Each member illustrates that personal trait seen as a shortcoming.

Group Discussion:

Members present their illustrated personal trait and tell why they are unhappy with it. Then, members exchange traits, exploring how the other person's perceived shortcomings could be alternatively seen as a desirable trait to others.

Members describe specific situations where these traits would be assets. Exchanges continue until no one is left with their original illustration.

Group members are often surprised at how positively their own perceived shortcomings are viewed by others. This exercise is effective with groups in any stage of development, as long as members can think abstractly.

Exercise 10

ROUGH JOURNEY

Purpose:

1. To compare life experiences.
2. To give feedback about individual achievement.
3. To enhance problem-solving skills.

Materials:

One photocopy of the illustration for each member; pens, pencils, crayons, or markers.

Description:

A. A brief discussion focuses on the obstacles to reaching our life goals and how these goals are often modified.
B. While handing out materials, the leader asks members to recall a personal goal that was attained despite much difficulty.
C. Members write the original goal in the "Start" box and the goal reached in the "Finish" box. Sometimes the two goals will differ.
D. In the corresponding box, members describe fears, self-doubt, or conflicts they may have experienced before reaching the final goal.
E. A line through the maze is drawn to best represent the sequence of events from "Start" to "Finish."

Group Discussion:

Each member describes what motivated them to set a particular goal. Fears, self-doubt, and/or interpersonal conflict are revealed in the order presented on the maze.

Each group member expresses what it felt like to finally achieve the goal. The members are encouraged to explain why their original goals might have been modified along the way. Other members are encouraged to comment, and to offer support and empathy.

This exercise is designed for well-integrated groups capable of abstract reasoning.

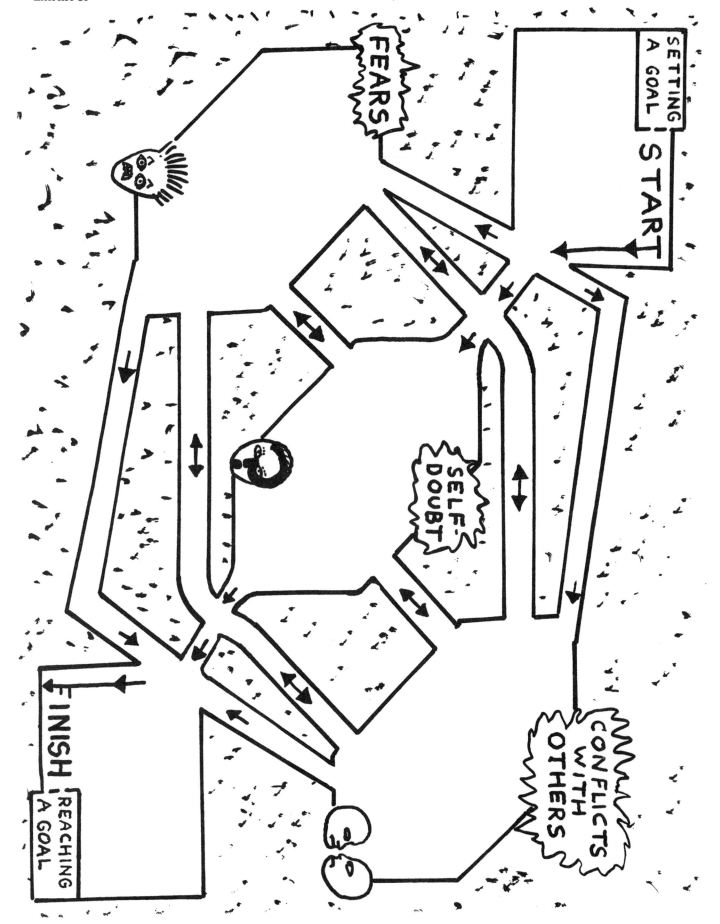

Exercise 11

BIG DOOR IN, SMALL DOOR OUT

Purpose:

1. To provide an opportunity for sharing how we deal with disappointment.
2. To recognize that many problems are universal.
3. To promote support and empathy.

Materials:

One photocopy of the illustration for each member; crayons, markers, pens, or pencils.

Description:

A. The group leader describes "Big door in, small door out" as a metaphor for situations that are easy to get into, but almost impossible to get out of.
B. Members are given the illustration. They are told to reflect on personal experiences to which the metaphor applies.
C. At the "IN" door, each member depicts how simple it was to become part of a given situation.
D. At the "OUT" door, each member depicts why it became so difficult to leave that same situation.

Group Discussion:

One member describes in detail how easy it was to enter the depicted situation. Others are asked to reveal if they would have been attracted to this situation under the same or similar circumstances. The complications of leaving this situation are described. The group identifies how this challenge led to feelings such as anger or frustration.

The leader asks whether or not the member escaped the situation, and how he or she dealt with the outcome. This procedure is repeated until all group members discuss their illustrations. This exercise is effective with groups in all stages of development, and any group type, as it can be interpreted on many levels.

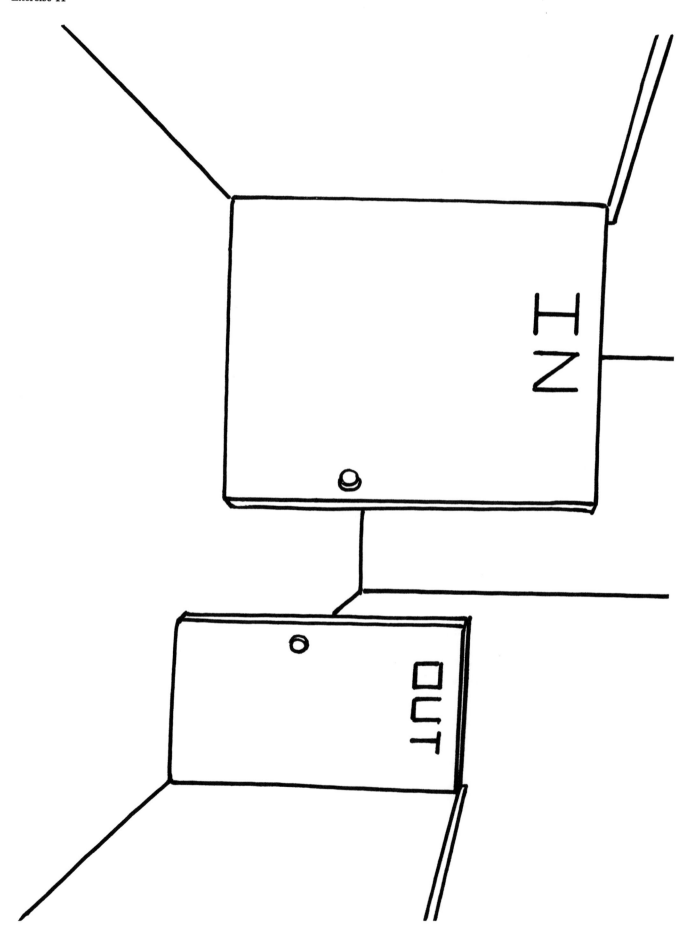

Exercise 12

LOOK!

Purpose:

1. To share personal experiences.
2. To understand the significance of events.

Materials:

One photocopy of the illustration for each member; pens, pencils, crayons, or markers.

Description:

A. The leader distributes the materials, and asks for feedback about what the illustration represents. The group is told that this exercise is open-ended and nonspecific.
B. Members are told to draw in what they imagine the two people standing at the window are seeing.

Group Discussion:

Members share their illustrations, describing what is going on outside of the window. They also explore how the two people at the window feel about what they are seeing. Members share their own experiences related to the illustration.

The group is encouraged to discuss what this might reveal about each member. Members may reveal important experiences or situations that have taken place in their lives.

This exercise works well with all group types in all stages of development, as it may be interpreted on many levels.

Exercise 13

SWITCHING HATS

Purpose:

1. To identify the qualities that attract people to others.
2. To promote group feedback by sharing individual perceptions.

Materials:

One photocopy of the illustration for each member; crayons, markers, pens, or pencils.

Description:

A. The group leader encourages members to describe some of the positive qualities of people they admire.
B. The materials are handed out, and the leader asks group members to think about someone in the group they would like to be if they had the chance.
C. Within the hat, each member draws the person he or she would most like to be. Reasons for this choice are written on the back of the illustration.

Group Discussion:

Members reveal which individual they would like to be. They describe the qualities they admire about that person. The leader asks the group to interpret what each member's choice reveals about their own needs and values. Members are often pleased to hear reasons why others admire them.

This exercise can be interpreted on many levels. It is effective with a variety of groups at all stages of development.

Exercise 14

HELP WANTED!!

Purpose:

1. To understand the significance of personal traits.
2. To promote group feedback about staff performance.
3. To share viewpoints and perspectives.

Materials:

One photocopy of the illustration for each member; pens, pencils, crayons, or markers.

Description:

A. While handing out the materials, the group leader asks members to think about the personality characteristics and professional skills that would be desirable in selecting a new staff member to fill an imagined staff vacancy.
B. Members illustrate this in the space provided.

Group Discussion:

Members describe their "want ads," and give reasons why these characteristics would be required to do a good job. Members are encouraged to comment on the details given.

Similarities and differences in the choices of desired qualities will emerge. Members are asked to explore what these choices reveal about each other's needs.

The group leader might wish to keep a list of the traits described.

This exercise is effective with any group type in all stages of development as it may be interpreted on many levels.

Exercise 15

THE GIFT

Purpose:

1. To be responsive to other's needs.
2. To provide an opportunity to share feelings about what might be missing from each other's lives.
3. To promote empathy and support.

Materials:

One photocopy of the illustration for each member; crayons, pens, pencils, or markers; tape.

Description:

A. The members are shown the illustration and asked how it could be used to fill each other's unfulfilled needs.
B. At random, a member's name is drawn out of a hat.
C. Members are told to illustrate an unfulfilled need for the member whose name was chosen. They write what this is on the back of the illustration.
D. Each member folds their completed illustration along the three dotted lines and tapes it shut, forming a box.
E. Members are now given their "gifts."

Group Discussion:

Each member describes the gift received and says why they think it was chosen for them. Members are encouraged to tell whether they think these gifts are a good idea, and can be used to meet their needs. Other group members are encouraged to comment. Members are often surprised at how much insight fellow members have about each other's needs.

Because this exercise requires knowledge of one another's unfulfilled needs, it is most effective with groups well-acquainted with each other, in the later stages of group development.

A GIFT TO:

FROM:

Exercise 16

ONE BIG NEIGHBORHOOD

Purpose:

1. To compare rewarding life experiences.
2. To promote reminiscence.

Materials:

One photocopy of the illustration for each member; pens, crayons, or markers; stapler or tape.

Description:

A. The group leader asks members to think about places where they have lived. They are told to reflect on a specific neighborhood that had special meaning for them.
B. One by one, each member decides if the chosen neighborhood most closely resembled the city, the suburbs, or a farm and rural area.
C. The leader folds and fastens each drawing so that only one scene faces forward. Letters appear on top and bottom of the page as cues indicating where to fold. The paper is folded back at the "C's" for a city block. The paper is folded back at both pairs of "S's" so that only the suburban scene at the center appears. The paper is folded back at the "F's" to reveal a farm and rural locale.
D. Members illustrate what made this chosen type of neighborhood special to them.
E. When illustrations are completed, the group leader tapes the illustrations together so that all the city scenes are together, followed by all the suburban scenes, and followed by all the rural scenes, thus forming "One Big Neighborhood."

Group Discussion:

An imaginary cross-country trip is taken. At each picture, the illustrator is asked to elaborate on the importance of his or her chosen place. Members are encouraged to ask one another about significant events or relationships associated with the neighborhood.

This discussion often evolves into reminiscences. It is effective with a variety of groups, and is useful in early stages of group development as it relies on a non-threatening form of self-disclosure.

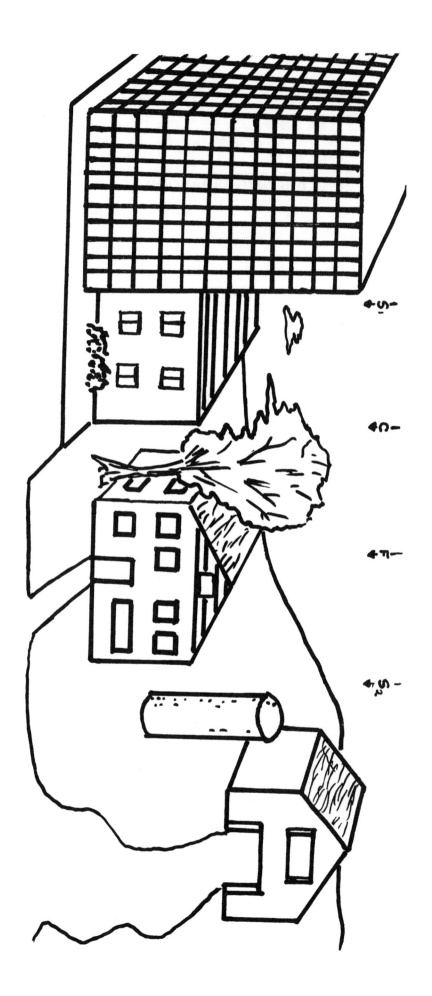

Exercise 17

THE BULLETIN BOARD

Purpose:

1. To help members become better acquainted.
2. To share information in a nonthreatening way.

Materials:

One photocopy of the illustration for each member; pens, pencils, crayons, or markers.

Description:

A. Members are shown the illustration and asked to think about the categories. They are encouraged to give examples of the kinds of information that might fit into each one.
B. The materials are distributed and members are told to check one category and to describe the details on the lines provided.

Group Discussion:

Members share their illustration. The leader might ask members who have filled in the same category to share their information together. Members are asked to comment on all the information being offered. Under the category "Problems needing the assistance of others," members are asked to help find solutions, and comment on the best way to help each other.

This exercise has many possible outcomes. Some members may use it as a concrete way to exchange information about events going on in the community. Others may need to reveal some personal information, and thus find this an opportunity for self-disclosure. Those members who choose "Problems needing the assistance of others," often reveal unfulfilled needs that should be addressed. This exercise is useful in groups that are newly formed, as it is nonthreatening and open-ended.

BULLETIN

CHECK ONE: ☐ PERSONAL ANNOUNCEMENT
☐ COMMUNITY AFFAIRS
☐ PROBLEM NEEDING ASSISTANCE

Exercise 18

HOLIDAY FEELINGS

Purpose:

1. To develop insight into feelings.
2. To understand viewpoints and perspectives.
3. To promote empathy between group members.

Materials:

One photocopy of the illustration for each member; pens, pencils, or crayons.

Description:

A. This exercise is to be used during an actual holiday week. (It is equally effective with any holiday.)
B. Photocopied illustrations are handed out during a general discussion of how holidays may or may not meet our expectations.
C. Each member fills in the line requesting the name of the holiday. Then, the members are asked to write in if it is a sad or happy occasion.
D. The paper is turned until the face with the corresponding feelings is right side up.
E. Now members are asked to illustrate something inside the circle that makes the holiday happy or sad to them.

Group Discussion:

Each member reads the statement indicating the holiday and its associated feeling. The leader directs others to explore in more detail the reasons for these feelings. Support and empathy are encouraged when someone has described sadness related to a holiday. It is suggested that at some point the discussion should explore whether we all have mixed feelings about holidays.

The degree of self-disclosure can vary with this exercise. This exercise is especially effective with people in a residential setting, since they often feel cut off from family and friends. It is effective with any group type at all stages of development.

Exercise 19

TRIPLE EXPOSURE

Purpose:

1. To follow directions and complete tasks.
2. To promote interaction.
3. To share viewpoints and perspectives.

Materials:

One photocopy of the illustration for each member; each color chart is photocopied for one third the number of people in the room. Crayons.

Description:

A. Group members are asked to follow directions closely, and are informed that the illustration is more than a simple "color by number exercise."
B. Everyone gets a copy of the illustration, but each member only receives one of the three color charts.
C. Members are asked to color illustrations according to the code of their color chart, regardless of what they think they see on the paper.

Group Discussion:

The leader invites members to verbalize different interpretations of the three pictures. Group members are encouraged to create stories about the depicted scenes.

Each member reveals how they think the person(s) in the picture feel(s) about the situation. One outcome is that members can relate interpretations of these drawings to personal experiences. Group members will be amused about the variety of pictures created.

This exercise is effective with any group type and may be used during all stages of group development.

COLOR BY LETTER CHART*

(People using this chart ignore all signs and numbers)

W = White
B = Black
N = Brown
R = Red
L = Blue

COLOR BY SIGN CHART*

(People using this chart ignore all letters and numbers)

− = Green
+ = Black
No Sign = Leave White

COLOR BY NUMBER CHART*

(People using this chart ignore all letters and signs)

1 = Yellow
2 = Blue
3 = Red
4 = Gray
5 = White

*For Exercise 19

Creative Therapy: 52 Exercises for Groups

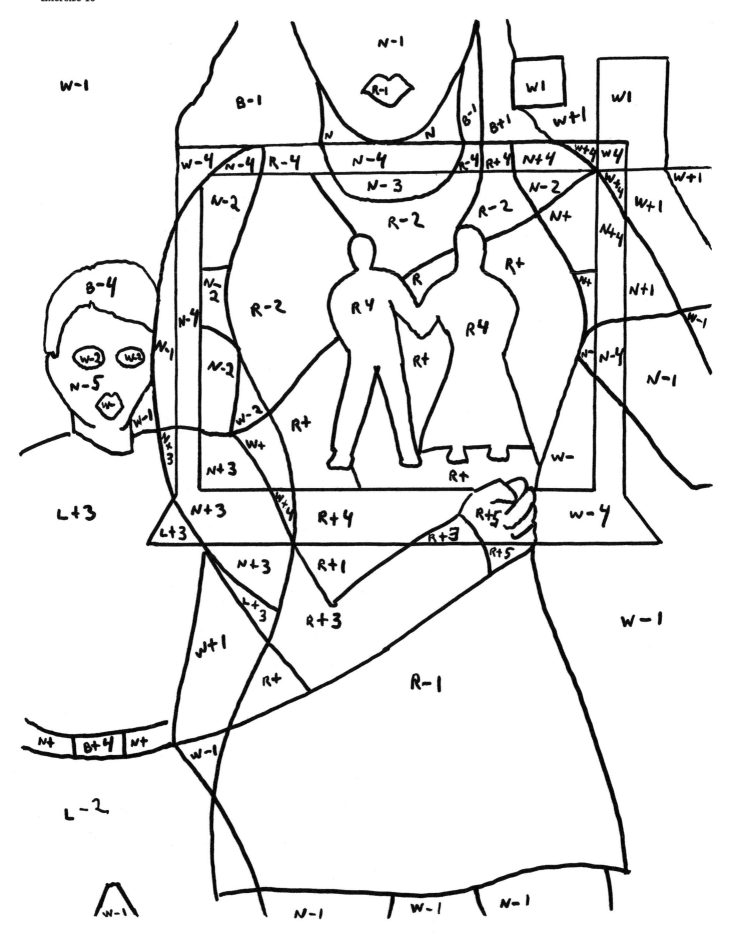

Exercise 20

SOMEONE TO BE PROUD OF

Purpose:

1. To describe the significance of other people in our lives.
2. To share viewpoints and perspectives.
3. To promote group cohesion and bonding.

Materials:

One photocopy of the illustration for each member; pens, pencils, markers, or crayons.

Description:

A. The group leader introduces the theme by having members explore reasons that people might feel proud of one another.
B. The group leader hands out the materials and asks members to illustrate a group member or other person in their life they are proud of.

Group Discussion:

Members share their illustration. They describe a person they are proud of, and what they think are that person's best attributes. Members are asked to interpret each other's choices, and their significance. Other members are encouraged to add whether they too would be proud of the person being described.

This exercise gives the group an opportunity to express positive feelings about one another, and is effective with any group type in all stages of development.

Exercise 21

MEETING AT THE CORNER

Purpose:

1. To express oneself through role-playing.
2. To promote a better understanding of group dynamics.
3. To encourage social interaction.

Materials:

One photocopy of the illustration for each member; pens, pencils, markers, or crayons; stapler or tape.

Description:

A. Members are asked to imagine socializing at one of four places: (a) a cafe, (b) a community center, (c) the park, or (d) a costume party.
B. As each member receives a paper, the leader asks at which location he or she would like to meet other people. The corner for that scene is folded over backward by the leader and fastened closed.
C. Each member holds the sheet so that only the chosen location is showing. Alongside this picture members write in an imagined conversation they might have at such a location.
D. The leader allows ample time for four consecutive discussions to take place.

Group Discussion:

All participants who chose the same location are asked to regroup and discuss among themselves what is on their paper. When each discussion ends, those people return to their seats. The members who chose the next location regroup and talk.

For each discussion, comments and questions are initiated only by those members sharing the chosen location. Other members of the larger group are asked to be silent and observant.

The leader's role is to make sure all members of each location get their chance to express the thoughts written on their paper. (This should be done in an indirect manner by asking members of each location to include those who have not yet spoken.)

This exercise is effective with virtually all group types in all stages of development because it is a nonthreatening opportunity for role-playing. It is a useful method by which members in newly formed groups become better acquainted.

Exercise 22

THE ALIEN

Purpose:

    1. To provide an opportunity for nonthreatening self-expression.
    2. To share viewpoints and perspectives.

Materials:

One photocopy of the illustration for each member; pens, pencils, crayons, or markers.

Description:

    A. The group leader introduces the theme by asking members to reflect on some of the shortcomings of the world that they live in.
    B. They are asked to describe both tangible and intangible things they think are needed by the planet earth.
    C. While passing out the materials, the leader asks for input as to how the picture relates to the theme.
    D. Members are told to fill in a description of what gift(s) a space alien should give the planet earth to best benefit mankind.

Group Discussion:

Members share both their illustration and the reasons they chose that gift(s). The group leader encourages members to explore the significance of their choices and what it (they) may reveal about how the member defines the world's problems. Similarities in gifts to the planet are focused on.

Though this exercise is effective with all stages of group development, it is recommended for groups in the earlier stages as it is relatively nonthreatening.

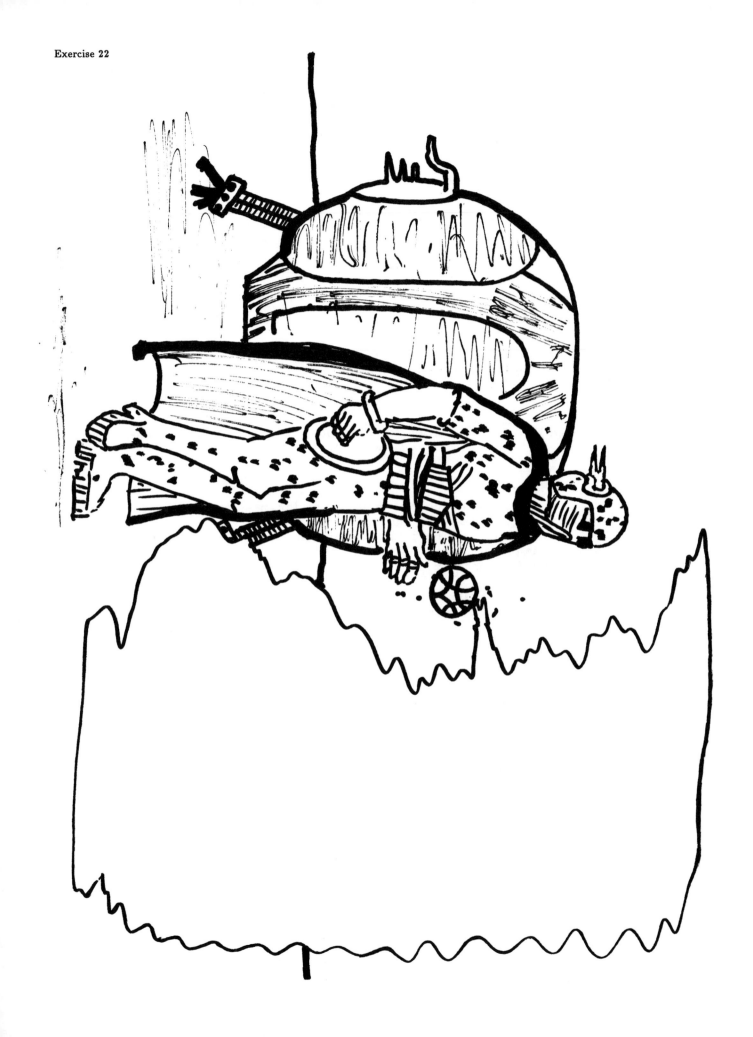

Exercise 23

ACTIONS SPEAK LOUDER THAN WORDS!!

Purpose:

    1. To understand interpersonal dynamics.
    2. To focus on the relationship between actual behavior and words.
    3. To promote the expression of conflict in an accepting environment.

Materials:

One photocopy of the illustration for each member; pens, pencils, or crayons.

Description:

    A. An individual's behavior, or actions, often communicates more than what the individual says. Group members explore this idea while materials are distributed.
    B. Members are asked to recall an incident or experience in which someone's behavior gave a totally different message than what had actually been said. What the individual said is written on the left side of the illustration.
    C. The contradicting behavior is drawn in the box below the word "Action."
    D. The real message that resulted from the depicted situation, is written on the right side.

Group Discussion:

The spoken words, the "Action," and the real message are read to the group by each member. Members are encouraged to offer feedback about each depicted situation, as well as to exchange views on whether they too would have interpreted the "real message" in the same way.

Members also explore the feelings related to each incident bearing a "double message." Members may reveal current or past situations where fellow group members' actions were different than their actual words.

This exercise can be an effective method by which members may express conflict in an accepting and supportive environment. It requires the ability for insight and abstract reasoning. It is recommended for all stages of group development.

Exercise 24

IT'S IN THE CARDS

Purpose:

    1. To explore fantasies as an expression of one's needs.
    2. To share concerns about the future.

Materials:

One photocopy of the illustration for each member; pencils, crayons, or markers.

Description:

    A. The group leader introduces a discussion of the fascination many people have with seeing into the future.
    B. The materials are distributed and the leader asks the members to think about how the illustration relates to the theme.
    C. Members draw in their own expectations for the future in each corresponding card.

Group Discussion:

Each member shares his or her illustration. Individual members describe how these projected future events could change their lives.

Group members explore what each other's expectations represent. They offer suggestions about how these can be achieved, and what measures might be taken to avoid any future disappointments. Feelings of pessimism and optimism will emerge and should be focused on.

This exercise is effective with groups that have established some degree of trust between each other and are in the later stages of development.

Exercise 24

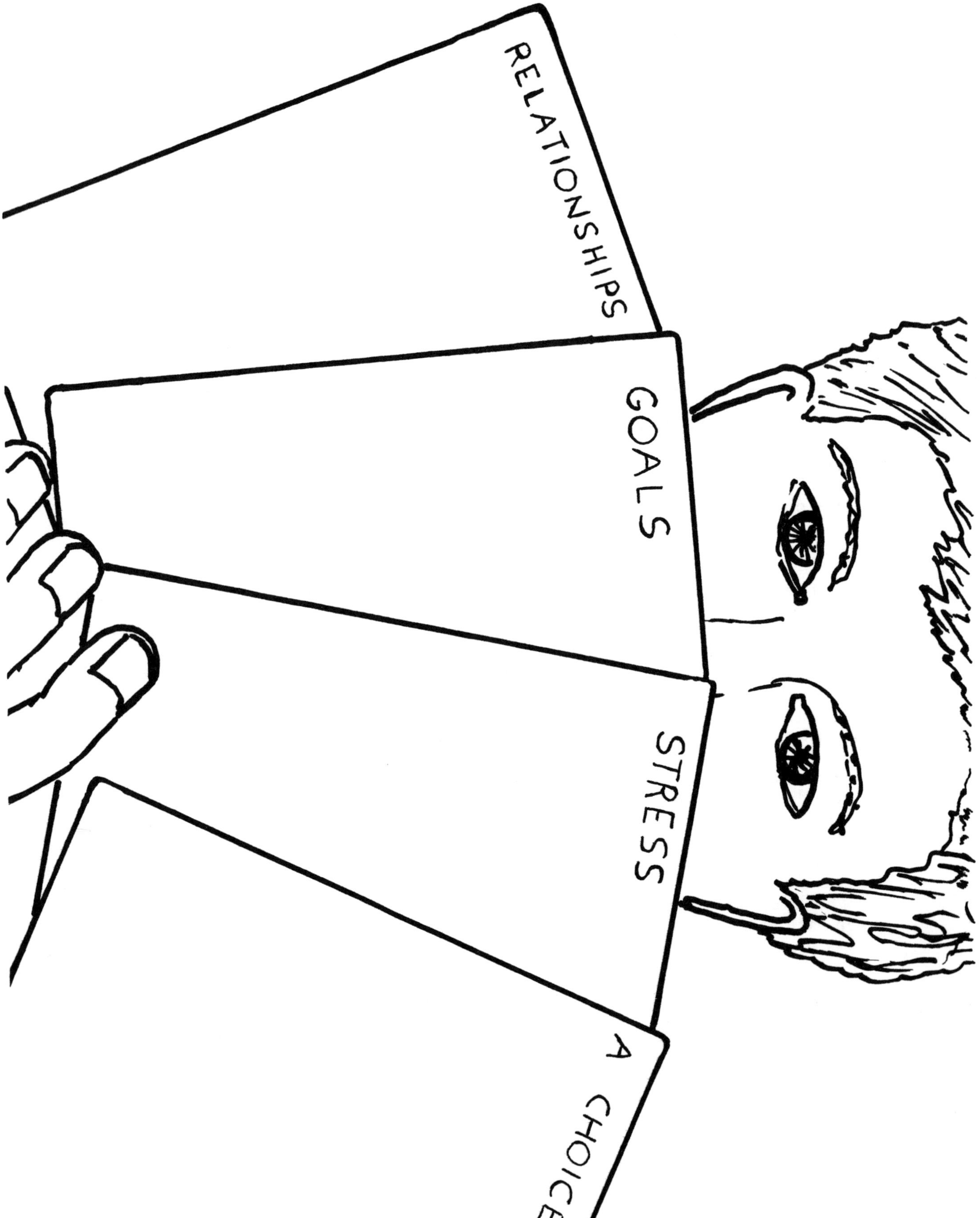

Exercise 25

TEARS

Purpose:

1. To promote feedback regarding perceptions of self and others.
2. To clarify and recognizing feelings.
3. To enhance group cohesion through self-disclosure.

Materials:

One photocopy of the illustration for each member; crayons, markers, pens, or pencils.

Description:

A. The leader asks members to think about how tears can reflect many kinds of emotions. Members are asked to describe how seeing others cry makes them feel.
B. The leader hands out the materials and asks members to illustrate the reason that this person is crying, and describe who it is.

Group Discussion:

Each member shares his or her illustration, describing who this individual is. The leader encourages group members to explore the experience or situation that led to the tears on the face.

In some instances, members may reveal actual conflicts or problems with which they themselves are struggling. This can be an opportunity for members to reveal troubling emotions, feelings, or experiences (and occasionally a way for members to help each other resolve difficulties).

Because of the self-revelation inherent in this exercise, it is most often effective in the middle to later stages of group development.

Exercise 26

THE CRYSTAL BALL

Purpose:

1. To identify and interpret individual needs.
2. To understand how feelings relate to expectations.
3. To share viewpoints and perspectives.

Materials:

One photocopy of the illustration for each member; crayons, markers, pens, or pencils.

Description:

A. The group leader encourages members to reveal some of their hopes and dreams for the future.
B. As materials are distributed, the members are asked to comment on how the picture of the crystal ball relates to the theme of this exercise.
C. Within the crystal ball, members illustrate what they think their future may hold for them.

Group Discussion:

Each member shares their imagined future with the group. Members are asked to comment on the significance as well as how realistic they feel these individual futures are.

Members are encouraged to provide constructive advice and suggestions about how these futures can be achieved or avoided if possible. This exercise gives members an opportunity to offer constructive advice to each other, and to share viewpoints.

This exercise is effective with group members that are well-acquainted with each other, in the middle to later stages of group development.

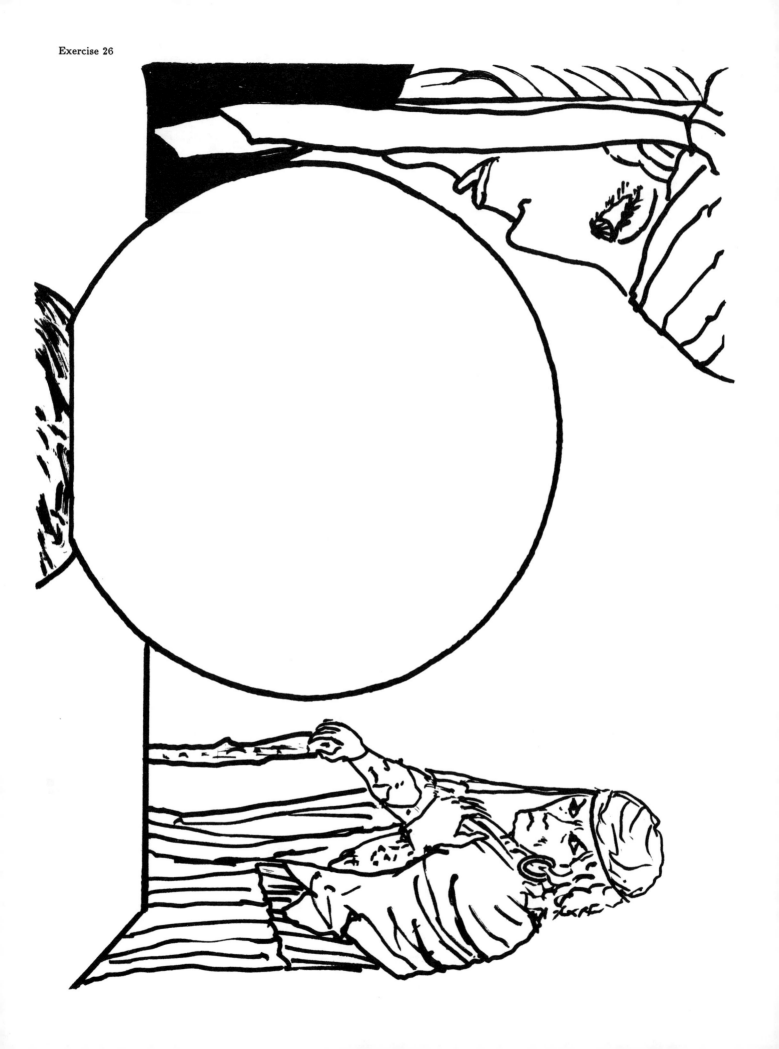

Exercise 27

REMOTE CONTROL

Purpose:

1. To identify individual areas of concern.
2. To promote trust and support for one another.
3. To recognize the potential to gain control over more aspects of our lives.

Materials:

One photocopy of the illustration for each member; crayons, markers, pens, or pencils.

Description:

A. While distributing materials, the leader talks about the common experience of feeling that "things are out of control."
B. Members are told that their illustration should focus on a current out-of-control situation, as well as a possible way of actually gaining control.

Group Discussion:

Each member describes both the current out-of-control situation, and the way they might gain control of it. Then they reveal to the group the likelihood of actually being able to do this. Members are encouraged to offer suggestions and support. Members focus on any similarities in the illustrated out-of-control situations, and are encouraged to exchange viewpoints and comments about the varied ways of gaining control.

A possible outcome of this exercise is that members may find ways of dealing effectively with problems of immediate concern to them. This exercise is effective with groups in the middle to later stages of development.

Exercise 28

FOLLOW IN MY FOOTSTEPS

Purpose:

1. To explore the dynamics of interpersonal learning.
2. To share viewpoints and perspectives.

Materials:

One photocopy of the illustration for each member; pens, pencils, crayons, or markers.

Description:

A. The group is asked to determine what is meant by the expression "follow in my footsteps."
B. Materials are distributed as the leader informs group members they can choose one of the two scenarios for this exercise: (a) How they would expect someone to follow in their own footsteps, or (b) How another person the member knew followed in someone else's footsteps.
C. In each illustrated "footstep," members draw a separate trait, behavior, characteristic, or attitude of one person that was adapted by another person.

Group Discussion:

Those who chose scenario "a" describe why the illustrated steps are necessary for someone to "follow in their footsteps." The group decides who among its own members might best follow such a scenario.

Those who chose scenario "b" describe how it felt when they first noticed someone imitating the traits, behaviors, characteristics, or attitudes of another person. The group should then be encouraged to explore how this person's change affected their relationship with that group member.

This exercise is intended for groups in all stages of development as it gives members an opportunity to explore how they think people learn from one another.

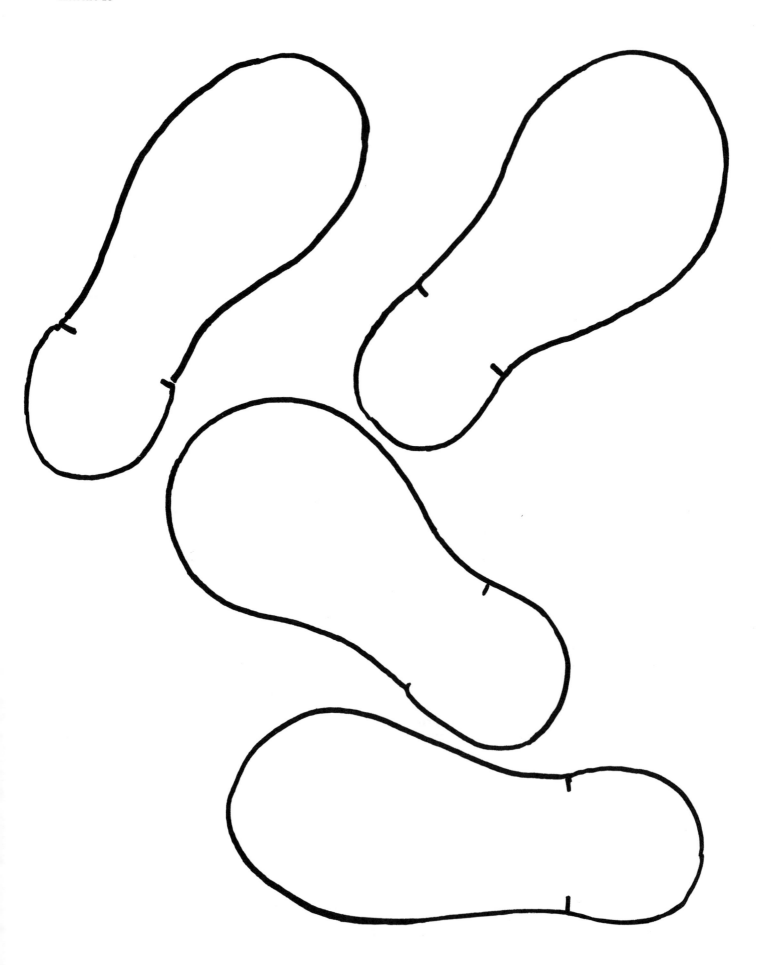

Exercise 29

THE BROKEN HEART

Purpose:

1. To compare life experiences.
2. To give empathy and reassurance.
3. To risk-take through self-disclosure.

Materials:

One photocopy of the illustration for each member; pens, pencils, crayons, or markers.

Description:

A. The leader shows the illustration to the group and asks them what they think the picture represents.
B. While handing out the materials, the group discusses how upsetting experiences "break" our hearts.
C. In the center of the illustration, members draw what experience or situation caused them to have a "broken heart."
D. On the back of the paper, they illustrate how they dealt with this situation or experience.

Group Discussion:

Members describe their individual illustrations, revealing what led to the situation or experience that "broke" their heart. Members reveal how they dealt with this upsetting experience, and if they feel they did so constructively.

Members are encouraged to be supportive and ask questions about the experience and relationships revealed. Members are asked if they would re-live the same experience again regardless of the outcome.

This exercise encourages members to reveal many types of negative experiences and situations in a supportive environment. It is effective with groups that have established some degree of trust between members, and are in the later stages of group development.

Exercise 30

YOU CAN LEAD A HORSE TO WATER BUT YOU CAN'T MAKE IT DRINK

Purpose:

1. To explore how individual expectations represent needs.
2. To exchange views on how we deal with disappointment.

Materials:

One photocopy of the illustration for each member; pens, pencils, crayons, or markers.

Description:

A. The group leader shows the illustration and asks for feedback about the meaning of the proverb "You can lead a horse to water but you can't make it drink."
B. While handing out the materials, the group leader has members reflect on how this proverb relates to unsuccessful attempts the group members have made in the past at changing the direction of another person's life or a personal situation.
C. Members illustrate the desired outcome in the depicted horse's trough. The situation that could not be changed is depicted in the horse's cart.

Group Discussion:

Members share their illustration. They are asked to describe how the depicted situation or person might have been better off if the desired change would have been accomplished.

Members explore whether these desired changes were realistic. Group members share their feelings about unsuccessful attempts at influencing others.

This exercise is most effective with groups that are capable of abstract reasoning, in all stages of development.

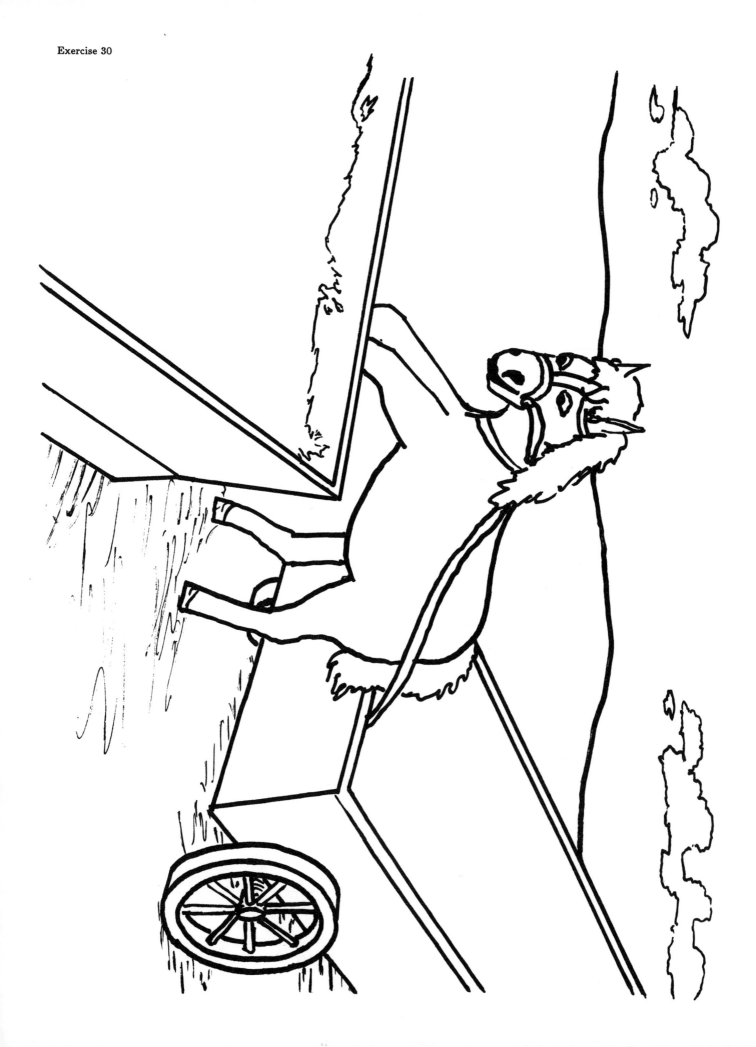

Exercise 31

THE HELPING HAND

Purpose:

1. To promote self-disclosure.
2. To build trust.
3. To reassure members that they can help each other.

Materials:

One photocopy of the illustration for each member; pens, pencils, markers, or crayons.

Description:

A. The leader introduces a discussion about the importance of people helping one another.
B. Members are asked to describe some general situations where people might need help.
C. While the leader distributes the illustrations, group members are asked to think of an area, a mood, or an emotion in which they might benefit by receiving help from others. They are told to write this on the back of the exercise page.
D. The descriptions are signed and re-distributed at random.
E. Each member reads what is written on the back of the page received. Within the illustrated "Helping Hand," they draw in the assistance they would offer or suggest to the group member. At this point, illustrations are then returned to the original member.

Group Discussion:

Members share their original illustration. The member who offered the helping hand describes what he or she drew, and the reasons for it. Often, members are encouraged to offer each other advice. Situations will differ but common themes will emerge and should be focused on.

Through this exercise, troubling emotions, feelings, or situations may be revealed. The group should be encouraged to follow-through on other ways they can continue to help each other. This exercise is effective during all stages of group development, with any group type.

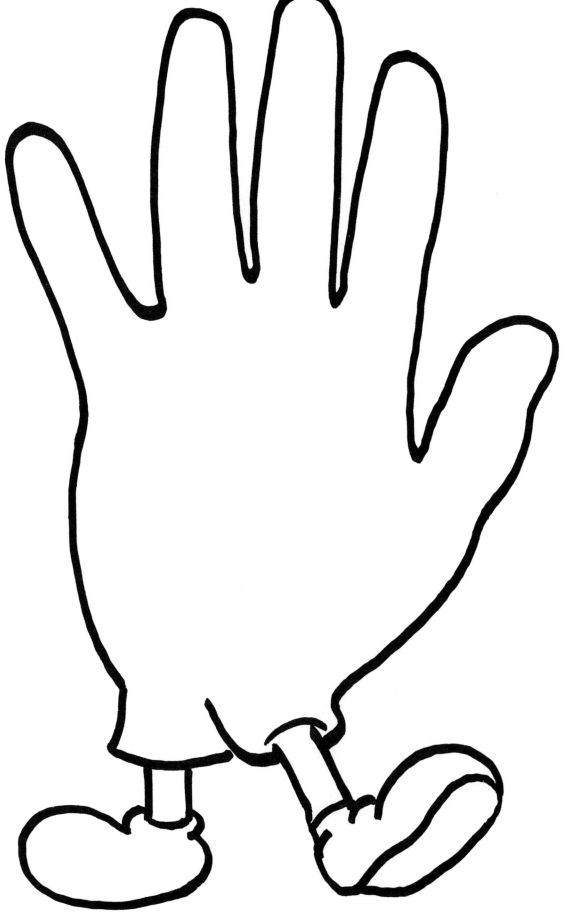

Exercise 32

GREAT EXPECTATIONS

Purpose:

1. To identify and interpret individual needs.
2. To promote recognition of the common bond between group members.

Materials:

One photocopy of the illustration for each member; pens, pencils, markers, or crayons.

Description:

A. A discussion is initiated about everyone's first reactions to being part of a group.
B. While the materials are being distributed, members are encouraged to talk about the meaning of the word "expectations," and how this word relates to the group process.
C. Members are asked to write in the space provided on the illustration (left side) their initial expectations when they first joined the group.
D. Next, members fill in the spaces corresponding to the categories of fulfillments (upper right) and disappointments (lower right) in the group.

Group Discussion:

The group leader has each member share their group expectations and fulfillments. Other members are encouraged to comment on their choices and the similarities between members. Members are encouraged to describe what they think each expectation reveals about their own needs. Group members share the fulfillments received from the group experience. It is interesting to explore why some members share similar rewarding feelings about the group, and others do not.

The disappointments section is then shared by each member. The leader should pay close attention to these descriptions, as they might provide important guides to the focus of future group meetings. A list may be compiled as each group disappointment is revealed, so that if appropriate, members can propose ways to change these disappointments into fulfillments.

This exercise is effective with groups in the early and middle stages of development.

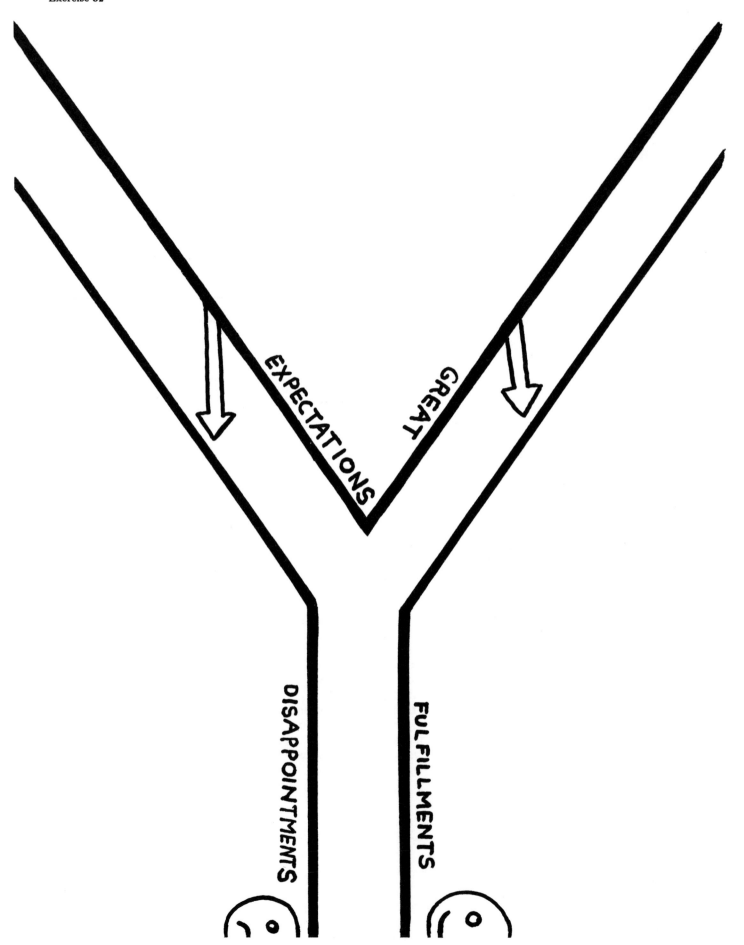

Exercise 33

THE MAGNIFYING GLASS

Purpose:

    1. To develop one's own insight.
    2. To use reminiscence as a learning experience.

Materials:

One photocopy of the illustration for each member; pens, pencils, crayons, or markers.

Description:

    A. A brief discussion is initiated about how personal experiences look different in retrospect. Members explore how difficult or troublesome incidents of the past are sometimes better understood today.
    B. While handing out materials, the leader asks members to recall past disturbing incidents that are now seen differently.
    C. Each member illustrates the troublesome incident on the surface beside the magnifier. In the magnifying glass itself, members draw how the whole experience looks much clearer today.

Group Discussion:

Each participant describes both parts of their illustration to the group. The leader encourages others to explore the reasons for the new understanding of the past incident. Members are encouraged to explore how factors such as emotional involvement, passage of time, changing outlook on life, and experiencing similar situations have led to increased insight.

This exercise begins as a reminiscence discussion and often evolves into a learning experience. It is effective with groups that can think abstractly. Group members should already be somewhat acquainted so they are not overly threatened by the level of self-disclosure.

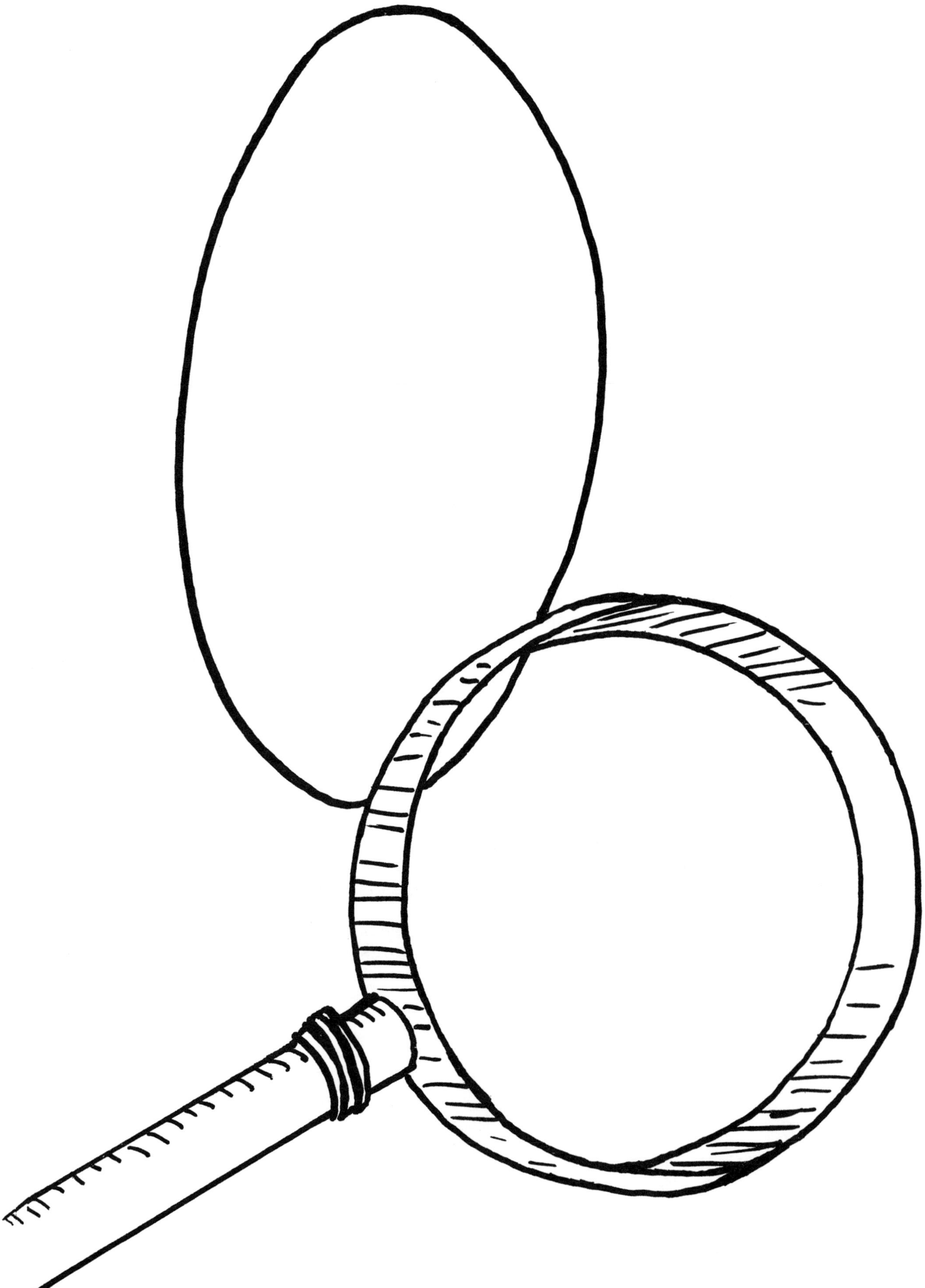

Exercise 34

THE OTHER SIDE OF THE COIN

Purpose:

1. To promote insight and empathy.
2. To encourage interpersonal learning.

Materials:

One photocopy of the illustration for each member; pens, pencils, crayons, or markers.

Description:

A. The leader encourages members to explore the meaning of the phrase, "The Other Side of the Coin." Materials are then distributed.
B. Members are asked to think of an unhappy situation in their lives. They illustrate it on the left coin beneath the phrase "One Side of the Coin," and then sign their names.
C. The illustrations are collected and re-distributed at random.
D. Each member examines the unhappy situation which someone else drew.
E. On the right coin, beneath the phrase "The Other Side Of the Coin," members illustrate what they think might be seen as a positive aspect or outcome of this depicted situation.

Group Discussion:

Papers are collected. For each drawing, the leader has the illustrator of the unhappy situation describe what he or she originally drew. Other members reveal and describe similar negative experiences.

Next, the illustrator of "The Other Side of the Coin" describes their interpretation of the positive aspect of this situation. The rest of the group is encouraged to comment about either side of the coin.

Acknowledging that others can help us discover positive aspects of difficult situations may stimulate greater self-awareness. This exercise is effective with many group types in all stages of development, as it may be interpreted on many levels.

Exercise 35

SAFEKEEPING

Purpose:

1. To reveal oneself through choice of objects.
2. To recognize the needs of others.

Materials:

One photocopy of the illustration for each member; pencils, pens, crayons, or markers.

Description:

A. The group leader encourages members to talk about why certain objects in one's life can have sentimental value, and may be symbolic of something important that took place on one's life.
B. Illustrations are folded in half like a greeting card, and distributed to members. The group leader asks members to think about any possessions or objects that were treasured by them. (This could be from the past or present.)
C. Members illustrate these possessions and objects on the inside of the folded safe.

Group Discussion:

Each member presents his or her illustration and describes the significance of each possession. Group members are encouraged to ask questions about the experiences or relationships these objects represent.

Often, this discussion evolves further because these treasured possessions may relate to the immediate needs of members.

Because of the open-ended nature of this exercise, it is effective with all group types in all stages of group development.

Exercise 36

BEST FOOT FORWARD

Purpose:

1. To incorporate group feedback into self-evaluation.
2. To encourage interpersonal bonding and group cohesion.

Materials:

One photocopy of the illustration for each member; crayons, markers, pens, or pencils.

Description:

A. The group leader introduces the idea that all of us have a great many strengths as well as weaknesses, and that we may have more strengths than we realize.
B. Members are then encouraged to discuss how personal strengths can emerge in a variety of situations. Example: solving a problem, making a wise purchase, meeting new people, and so on. (Members may focus on situations that have arisen in the group.)
C. Members' names are drawn at random out of a hat.
D. The materials are distributed. Members think about the person whose name they received, and draw in specific situations they think that person would excel in.

Group Discussion:

Members share their illustrations and disclose which member they are describing. Members describe whether they agree with these perceptions of themselves.

Each member has an opportunity to reveal what they think their "best foot forward" is. Members are often surprised at how positively others view them.

This exercise is effective with groups who are acquainted with each other, and is therefore useful in the middle and later stages of group development.

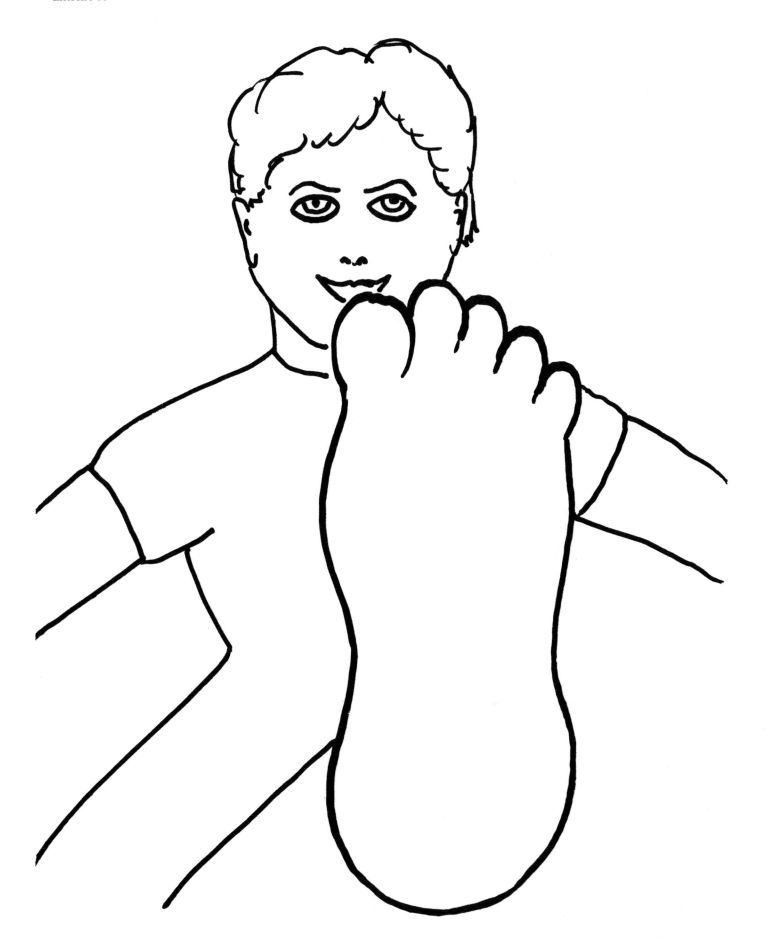

Exercise 37

CIRCLE CARTOON

Purpose:

1. To explore current individual concerns.
2. To develop insight.
3. To understand interpersonal dynamics.

Materials:

One photocopy of the illustration for each group member; pens, pencils, or markers.

Description:

A. As materials are distributed, the leader initiates a general discussion of the concept: "People don't always say what they're thinking."
B. Members are asked to think of an interaction with any staff member that is representative of this concept.
C. Each member completes the cartoon showing the words and thoughts communicated between staff and client.
D. Each member numbers the panels to best illustrate the progression of communication between the two people.

Group Discussion:

Each cartoon is read in the proper sequence. The illustrator tells why certain words, thoughts, and feelings were attributed to each person. The leader encourages others to ask any questions which will help everyone understand the dynamics involved.

This exercise requires a degree of abstract thinking and insight. It is therefore recommended for groups in later stages of development.

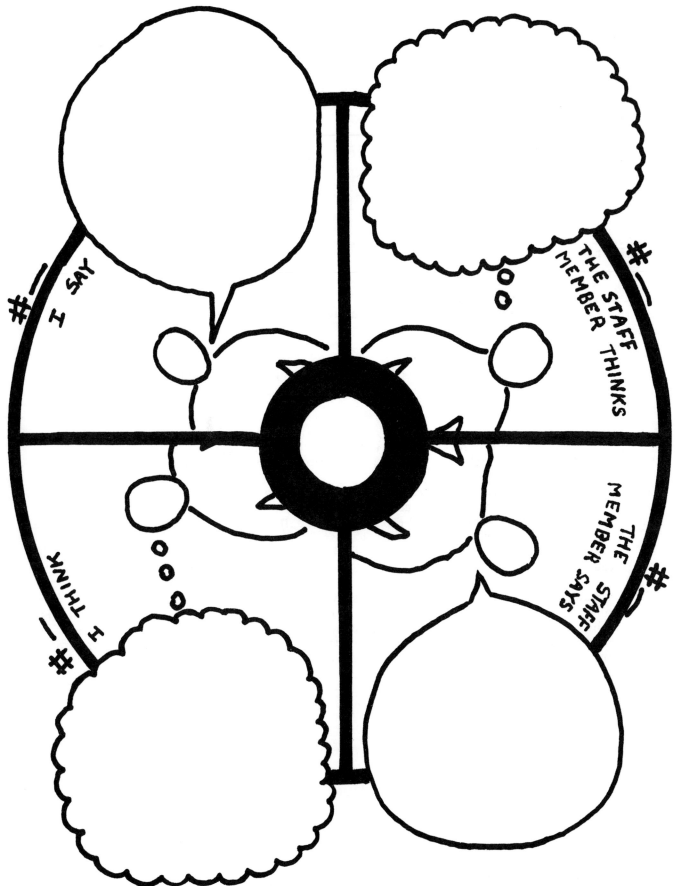

Exercise 37

CIRCLE CARTOON

Purpose:

1. To explore current individual concerns.
2. To develop insight.
3. To understand interpersonal dynamics.

Materials:

One photocopy of the illustration for each group member; pens, pencils, or markers.

Description:

A. As materials are distributed, the leader initiates a general discussion of the concept: "People don't always say what they're thinking."
B. Members are asked to think of an interaction with any staff member that is representative of this concept.
C. Each member completes the cartoon showing the words and thoughts communicated between staff and client.
D. Each member numbers the panels to best illustrate the progression of communication between the two people.

Group Discussion:

Each cartoon is read in the proper sequence. The illustrator tells why certain words, thoughts, and feelings were attributed to each person. The leader encourages others to ask any questions which will help everyone understand the dynamics involved.

This exercise requires a degree of abstract thinking and insight. It is therefore recommended for groups in later stages of development.

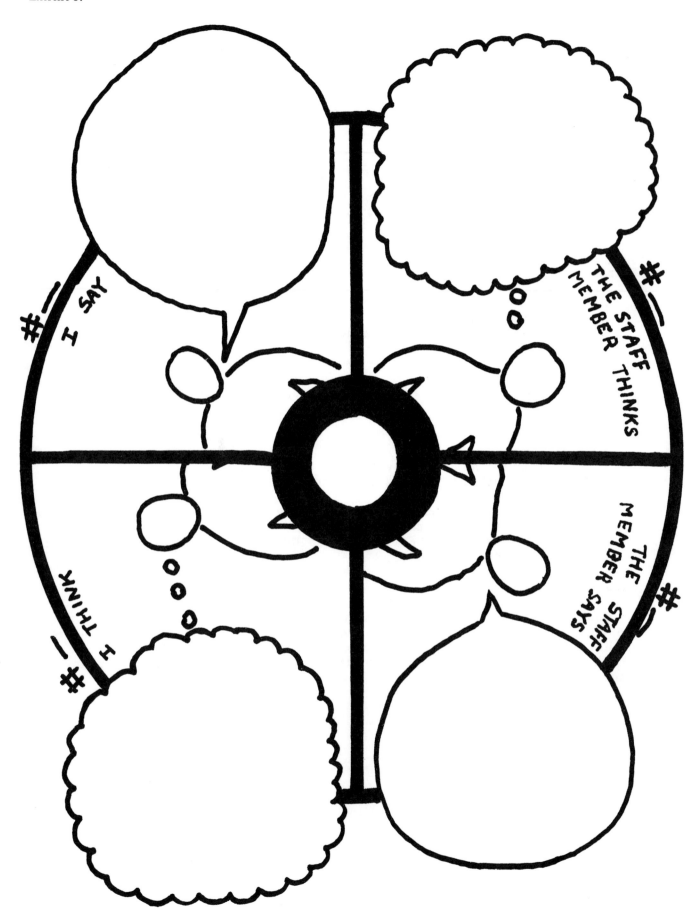

Exercise 38

GROUP LEADER'S AGENDA

Purpose:

1. To express oneself through role-playing.
2. To demonstrate to members how they can help one another.
3. To promote a better understanding of group dynamics.

Materials:

One photocopy of the illustration for each member; pens, pencils, crayons, or markers.

Description:

A. Members talk about why a group discussion of general interest and balanced input is preferred over a discussion in which people present individual concerns of limited interest to the group.
B. While distributing materials, the leader asks members to think about how they would run a group discussion to best involve as many people as possible, and to list their chosen topics in the box.
C. The group leader tells members that they can use any method that they think would be effective for running their group.
D. The room is divided into smaller subgroups.

Group Discussion:

Each member runs their subgroup for a few minutes, according to their own agenda. The staff member promotes discussion by offering leaders and participants support and encouragement. When discussions have ended, everyone in the room shares how it felt to take the role of leader. They explore the different methods used to promote group discussion, and try to determine which ones proved most effective (and why).

This exercise may help group members to become more aware of the kinds of effective interventions used by the staff in running the group. It is recommended for use with higher functioning groups in the later stages of development, as it can be stressful and demanding.

GROUP LEADER'S
AGENDA

Exercise 39

EVERY CLOUD HAS A SILVER LINING

Purpose:

1. To encourage self-disclosure.
2. To promote empathy and reassurance.

Materials:

One photocopy of the illustration for each member; pens, pencils, crayons, or markers.

Description:

A. The group leader distributes the materials and begins the exercise by asking members to fold their copies of the illustration over at the center line. Each paper is now an illustration of the cloud that can be opened (like a greeting card), to reveal blank paper.
B. Members are asked to describe what they think is meant by the saying "Every cloud has a silver lining."
C. Members are instructed not to open the flaps at this time, but to draw a distressing personal experience directly on the cloud. They are asked to sign their names.
D. Papers are collected, and re-distributed at random to other group members. On the blank space provided inside, members are asked to search for and illustrate any possible positive or comforting element to the distressing experience described. Then, they are asked to identify themselves with their signatures.

Group Discussion:

A discussion of each illustration between the two contributors is initiated. The negative experience - and the perceived positive component - are re-stated to the group by the leader. Other members are encouraged to offer additional reactions. Members might also explore whether identifying their names affected their participation in this exercise.

This exercise works best with groups whose members are perceptive and capable of abstract reasoning. It is designed for groups in the later stages of development.

Exercise 40

THE REPORTER

Purpose:

1. To provide an opportunity for one-to-one communication.
2. To share responsibility in order to complete a task.
3. To explore common needs to promote group identity and cohesion.

Materials:

One photocopy of the illustration for group members; pens, pencils, markers, or crayons.

Description:

A. Members are asked how they would feel being interviewed by a reporter seeking their opinions about the group.
B. Members are divided into pairs. One member is designated as the reporter; the other member is interviewed. The reporter writes down the answers the member gives to the questions asked.
C. Reporters are encouraged to add additional questions to the interview.

Group Discussion:

The reporters describe the information gained from the interviews held with the member. Members interviewed give feedback on how well their responses were understood. Other members are encouraged to comment and add to the interview being described. The leader has the group explore possible reasons behind the feelings expressed.

This exercise may help members talk about their opinions and feelings in an accepting environment. An outcome of this exercise is that the group can explore whether the revealed information might be used to actually make constructive changes in the group. Additionally, the group's dynamics and members' roles may become more apparent to the leader. This exercise is effective with all group types in all stages of development.

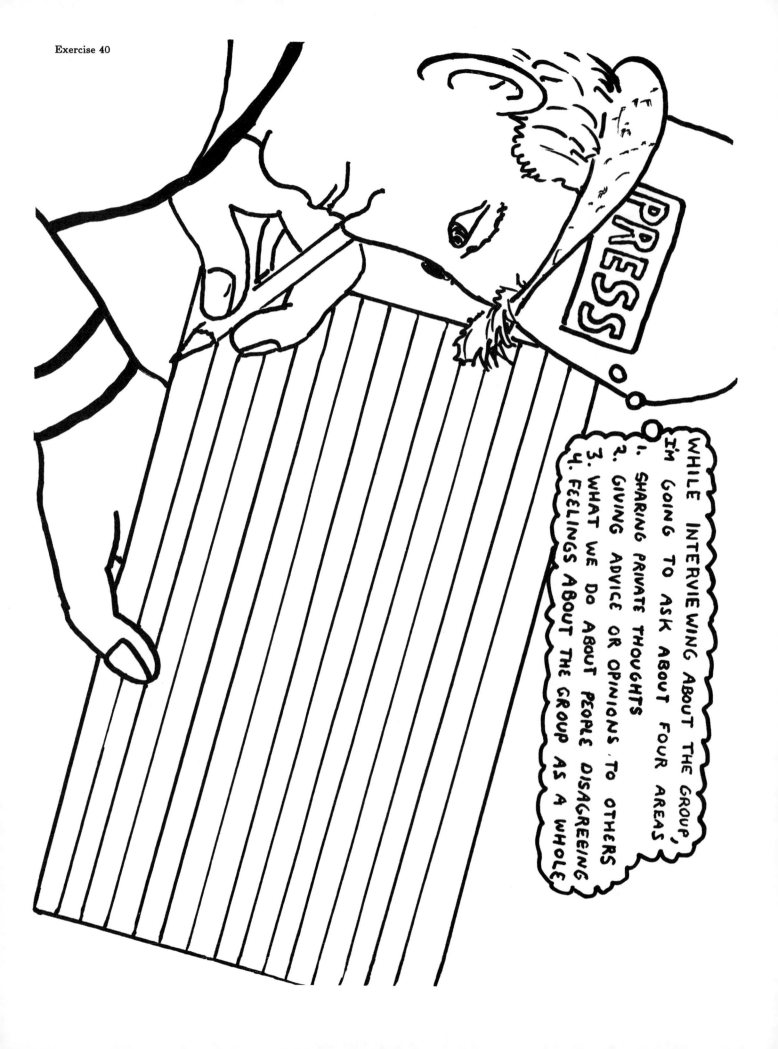

Exercise 41

BAILING OUT

Purpose:

    1. To recognize one's own limitations.
    2. To share viewpoints and perspectives.
    3. To compare life experiences.

Materials:

One photocopy of the illustration for each member; pencils, pens, crayons, or markers.

Description:

    A. Group members are asked to talk about what it means to "bail out" of a situation (when things get too tough).
    B. As materials are distributed, members give examples of situations that people might need to bail out of.
    C. Members illustrate in the space within the airplane a situation or experience that they've wanted to bail out of. This may be a current situation they're involved in, or one they've experienced in the past.
    D. In the space provided on the parachute, members are asked to illustrate how, in the past, they actually bailed out of this situation (or what they imagine, at present, might be the best way out).

Group Discussion:

Members share their illustration. They describe the experience or situation and the "bail out" chosen. Other members are encouraged to explore these choices through comments and questions.

The leader helps the group to identify feelings of anxiety, conflict, and so forth as each illustration is described.

As this exercise focuses on self-revelation, it is most effective with groups who are well-acquainted with each other, and have developed some degree of trust between members.

Exercise 42

COMING OUT OF YOUR SHELL

Purpose:

1. To incorporate group feedback into self-evaluation.
2. To develop insight about one's role in the group process.
3. To recognize each other's potential.

Materials:

One photocopy of the illustration for each group member; pens, pencils, crayons, or markers.

Description:

A. As group members are shown the illustration, they are asked to comment on what the saying "Coming out of your shell" means.
B. Materials are distributed.
C. The group leader asks group members to illustrate within the space provided, their impressions of a fellow group member who at some point in the past actually came out of his or her shell. If possible, the illustration should incorporate information about the point during the group process this occurred.

Group Discussion:

Members share their illustration. The leader should encourage others to comment and provide additional examples of how the member being described changed. In turn, the member being described is asked to comment on whether he or she agrees with the description, and to add how they feel about this analysis.

Group members are often surprised at how closely observed their behavior is by other members in the group. If appropriate, the group leader might seek suggestions on how members can help enhance the group atmosphere to encourage others to "come out of their shell."

This exercise is most effective when used with well-integrated groups during the later stages of group development.

Exercise 43

TURNING OVER A NEW LEAF

Purpose:

1. To incorporate group feedback into self-evaluation.
2. To provide an opportunity to clarify feelings about changing aspects of one's life.
3. To give and receive advice in order to better adjust to life situations.

Materials:

One photocopy of the illustration for each member, already folded at the dotted line; pens, pencils, crayons, or markers.

Description:

A. The group begins with a discussion of the proverb, "Turning over a new leaf."
B. While handing out materials, group members discuss the possibility of changing an aspect of their lives that is self-destructive or harmful to others. The leader tells the members to imagine exchanging one aspect of their lives.
C. In one illustrated leaf provided, each member draws in the circumstance or aspect of their life they want changed.
D. On the other illustrated leaf, they draw or write how an alternative behavior could be more constructive.

Group Discussion:

Each participant describes his or her completed drawing and tells why they want to make the perceived change. Members focus on how they can help each other work toward making these changes. The leader should help members explore why it is often difficult to change negative behavior.

This exercise is effective with virtually any group type at all stages of development because it may be interpreted on many levels.

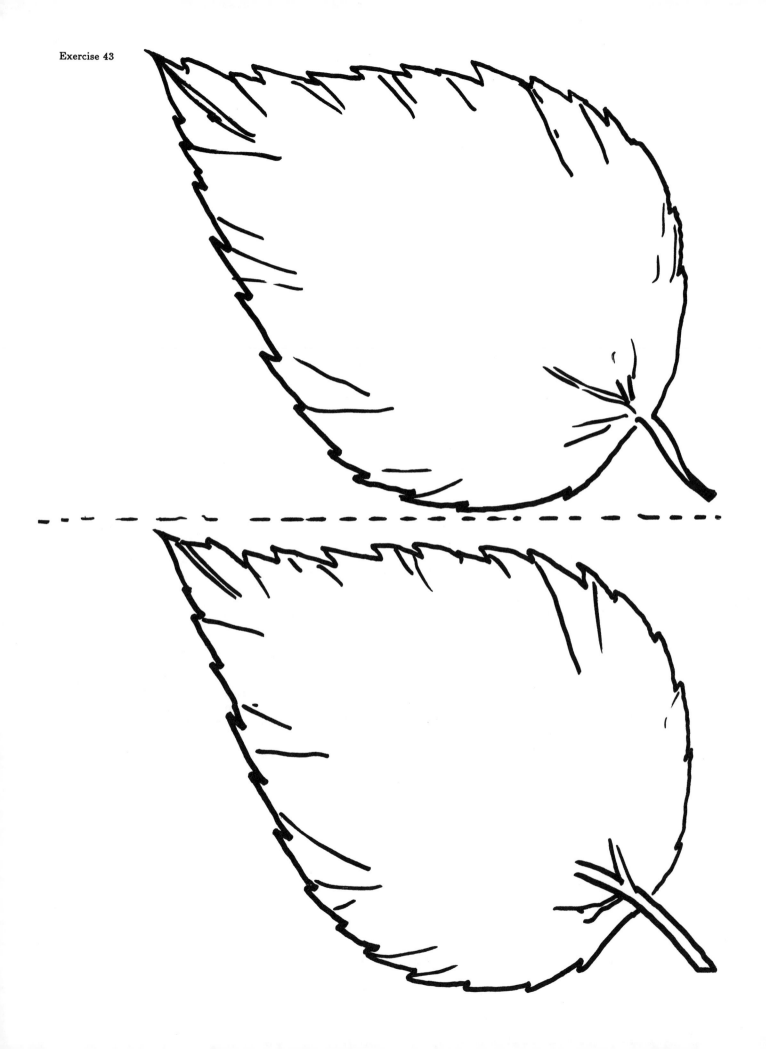

Exercise 44

THE INTRODUCTION

Purpose:

1. To incorporate group feedback into self-evaluation.
2. To recognize personal strengths.

Materials:

One photocopy of the illustration for each member; pens, pencils, crayons, or markers.

Description:

A. The group leader asks members to talk about how they would describe themselves to people they were meeting for the first time. Examples are given as materials are handed out.
B. Members are asked to fill in their word balloon, writing in what they think are the important aspects of themselves they would like to share during an introduction.

Group Discussion:

Members share their illustrations with the group and actually go through the motion of formally introducing themselves.

Group members are encouraged to ask questions, and if appropriate, add to the description of the member being introduced.

This exercise is effective with groups who are in the early stages of development, and may be an effective tool for groups whose members need to become better acquainted.

ALLOW ME TO INTRODUCE MYSELF

Exercise 45

THE GROUP QUILT

Purpose:

1. To evaluate one's own role in the group.
2. To understand group dynamics.
3. To promote group identity and cohesion.

Materials:

One photocopy of the illustration for each group member; crayons, markers, pens, or pencils.

Description:

A. The group leader initiates a discussion about what it means to have a role in a group process.
B. As materials are distributed, members discuss how individual roles add to the unique identity of the group in general.
C. Members are asked to illustrate on the quilt piece their individual roles, as they themselves see them, within the group.

Group Discussion:

After the members describe their roles in the group, the leader attaches the illustration sheets together to form a large rectangle. Group members may offer suggestions or comments on each other's specific roles.

The leader helps members to focus on how each group member adds to the group identity. When all members have shared their illustrations, the group "quilt" will be completed. By offering peer support and understanding, this exercise may help to encourage the quiet or guarded member to become more open. The group benefits from this exercise because of the insight gained about the individual's significance to the group process.

This exercise is effective with groups well-acquainted with each other, in the later stages of group development.

Exercise 45

Exercise 46

THE HOURGLASS

Purpose:

    1. To compare life experiences.
    2. To promote empathy and support.
    3. To encourage self-disclosure.

Materials:

One photocopy of the illustration for each team; pens, pencils, crayons, or markers.

Description:

    A. The group leader asks how an hourglass is often used to symbolize time passing in our lives.
    B. As materials are distributed, the concepts of time running out and having time left are also shared.
    C. In the portion of the illustration "A Long Way to Go," members are asked to illustrate experiences or aspects of their life that they feel they have more time (or enough time) left to accomplish.
    D. In the portion of the illustration marked "Time Ran Out," they are asked to draw what situation, experience, or aspect of their life occurred in which the time ran out.

Group Discussion:

The significance of both time running out and "A Long Way to Go," and what is revealed in each of these sections, is focused on. Members are encouraged to comment on what is being shared, and to ask questions about what each member described.

A result of this exercise is that members often reveal something they have not previously shared with each other. Members may describe less rewarding life experiences that they are glad are over. Other members may be supportive in helping the individual concentrate on more positive aspects of his or her life.

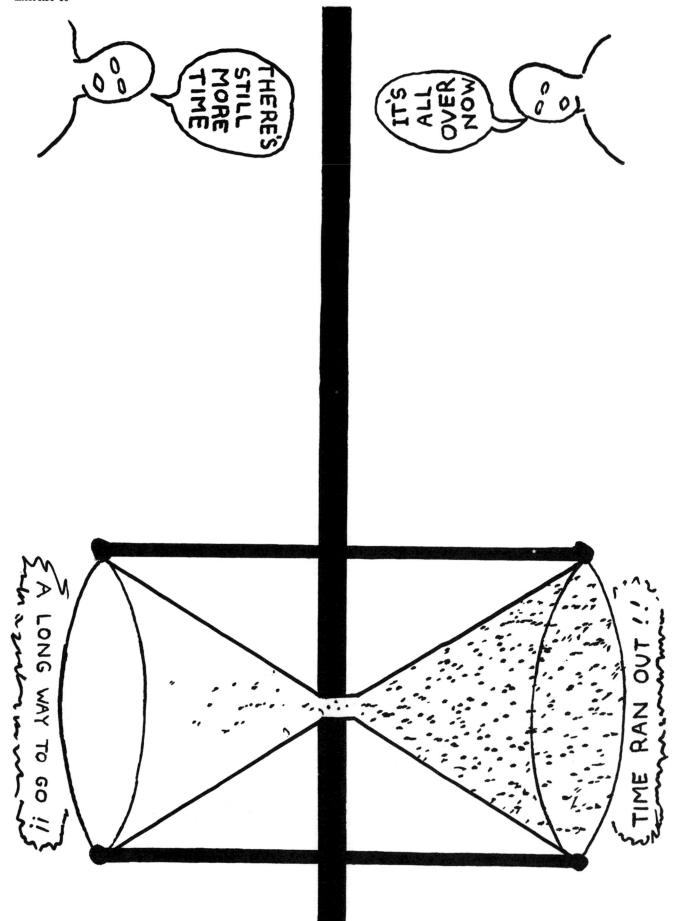

Exercise 47

THE VISITORS

Purpose:

1. To develop insight into the group process.
2. To share viewpoints and perspectives.
3. To promote group identity and cohesion.

Materials:

One photocopy of the illustration for group members; pens, pencils, markers, or crayons.

Description:

A. The positive and negative aspects of allowing people to observe the group process is discussed. Group members are asked how they might feel about visitors sitting in on a group.
B. Members are given the materials, and told to illustrate what they think the visitors might observe during their group session.

Group Discussion:

Members share their illustrations. Each member describes in detail what the visitors are observing in the group. The group leader should help members imagine what the visitor's comments might be. In addition, the group members should be encouraged to add their own comments to what the visitors are observing in each illustration.

This exercise affords members an opportunity to evaluate some of the positive and negative aspects of the group process, as well as fellow members' roles in it. By comparing the positive and negative aspects observed by the visitors, members are encouraged to find constructive ways to further develop the group process.

This exercise may be a useful tool in helping the leader to assess each individual member's group experience and group satisfaction. It is effective with groups in the middle to later stages of development.

Exercise 48

PAINTING YOURSELF INTO A CORNER

Purpose:

    1. To analyze a problem.
    2. To identify with others.
    3. To develop insight through group feedback.

Materials:

One photocopy of the illustration; blank sheets of paper the size of the illustration; markers or crayons.

Description:

    A. The group is asked to define what is meant by the expression "Painting Yourself into a Corner." Members are encouraged to give personal examples.
    B. After hearing several examples, the leader selects one person to re-state his or her own problem, and draw it alongside the person trapped in the corner of the illustration.

Group Discussion:

One by one, others interview this member in order to elicit additional contributing factors that helped "paint this person into a corner." Each new factor is represented on another floor tile (a blank sheet of paper).

All floor tiles are attached to the illustration of the man in the corner, so that a large rectangle is formed.

Members are asked to reflect on whether or not each problem could have been avoided. Leaders should also encourage discussion of similar situations among members.

This exercise is repeated as often as time permits. It works well with groups in later stages of development who are capable of abstract thinking.

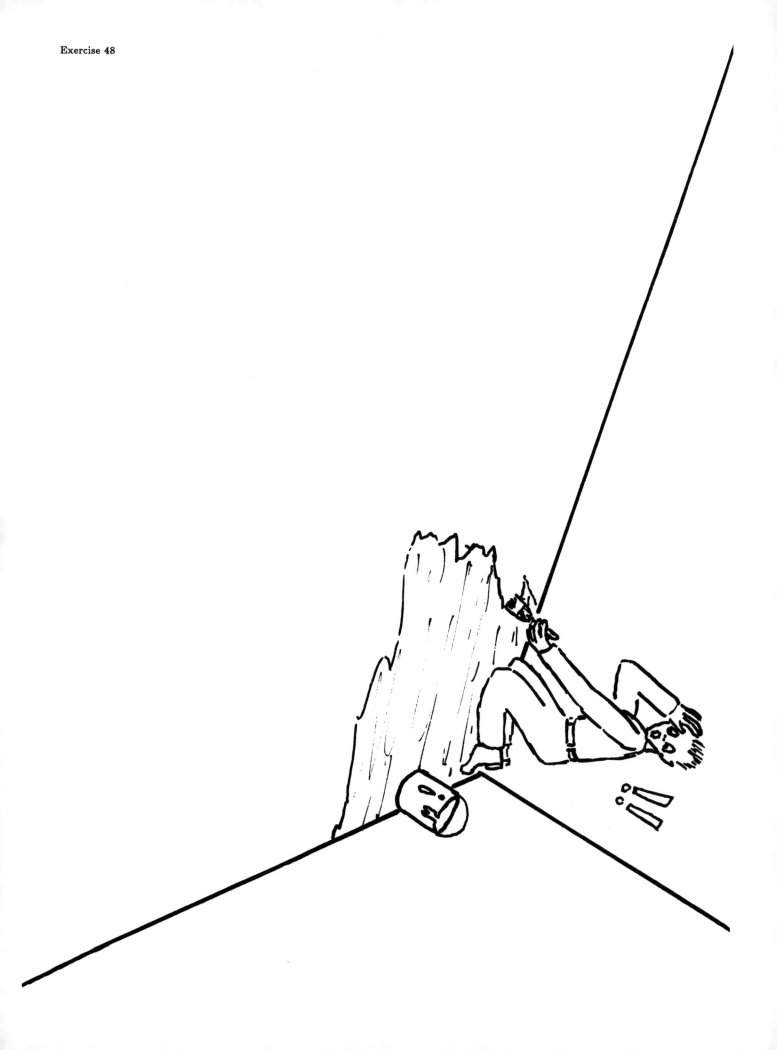

Exercise 49

THE GOOD AND BAD NEIGHBORS

Purpose:

1. To present individual concerns about living conditions.
2. To provide an opportunity for about open communication, and the expression of negative feelings.
3. To demonstrate universality through the recognition of common problems.

Materials:

One photocopy of the illustration for each member; pens, pencils, crayons, or markers.

Description:

A. The group discusses the positive and negative aspects of living in close proximity to others. This could be a shared room, an apartment building, a neighborhood, a school or a residential facility, and so on.
B. While the leader hands out the materials, members are asked to think about both the rewarding and annoying aspects of having neighbors.
C. They are asked to illustrate several things that represent some of the positive aspects in the windows of the "good" neighbor's house. They are then asked to illustrate some of the negative aspects in the windows of the "bad" neighbor's house.

Group Discussion:

Members share their illustrations, and contrast the qualities of the good and bad neighbors. The discussion may be wide-ranging, covering all aspects of living with neighbors. The benefits and drawbacks of good and bad neighbors will be included. Often, current conflicts and feelings about sharing common space or living with fellow members may arise during this exercise. Members may need to explore their frustrations and complaints about living conditions.

Because of the open-ended aspect of this exercise, it can be used with all group types. It is effective in both the early and later stages of development, and is a useful tool for sharing experiences.

SUGGESTION
BOX

Exercise 50

PRESCRIPTION FOR HAPPINESS

Purpose:

1. To encourage insight into each other's needs.
2. To share constructive advice.

Materials:

One photocopy of the illustration for each group member; pens, pencils, or crayons.

Description:

A. The leader begins the discussion by asking what is meant by a prescription.
B. While handing out the materials, group members discuss how everyone could benefit from a little more happiness.
C. Members names are drawn at random.
D. Members illustrate the prescription that would help make the chosen member feel happier and more content. Members are reminded to describe personal qualities as well as tangibles such as money.

Group Discussion:

Members share their drawings, and talk about their reasons behind the prescriptions for each other. Members are asked their reactions to the prescription suggested for them. Members ask each other how these prescriptions might change their lives.

Group members are encouraged to add comments to each other's prescriptions. Members are often surprised at the degree of insight others show into their individual needs.

This exercise is effective with groups in the later stages of development, and with members who are capable of abstract reasoning.

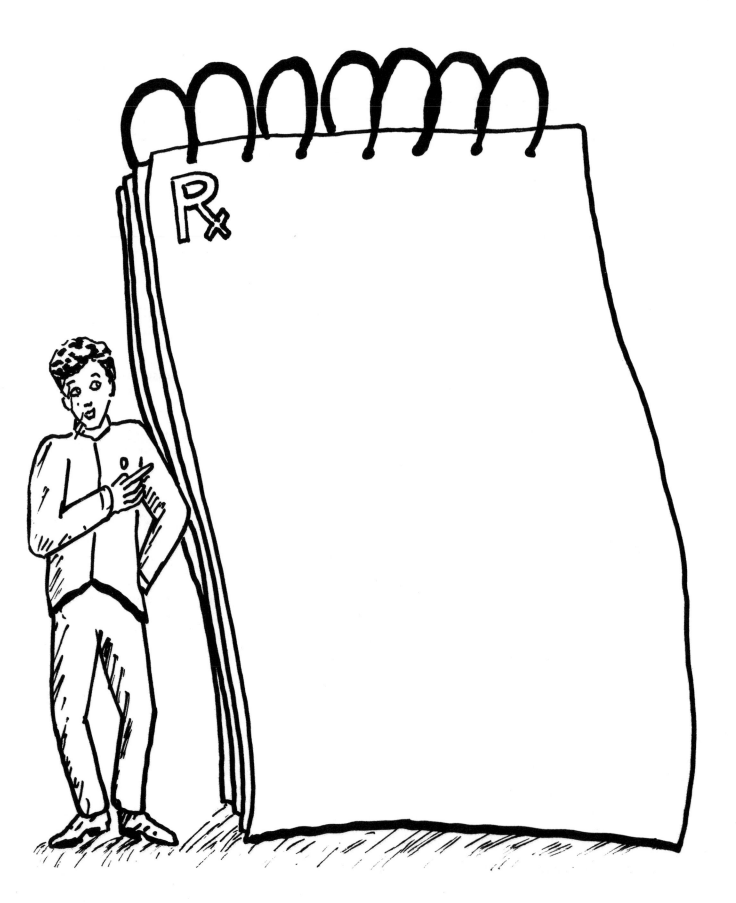

Exercise 51

THE SUGGESTION BOX

Purpose:

1. To promote group cohesion.
2. To develop problem-solving skills.

Materials:

One photocopy of the illustration for each member; pens, pencils, crayₒ
ers.

Description:

A. The leader introduces the idea of a suggestion box. Members are e
   comment on the opportunity of being able to make anonymous recomm
B. Materials are distributed, and members are asked to write an actual s
   improving the program, or something about their institution where
   takes place.
C. When completed, illustrations are folded (to insure anonymity) and
   the leader.

Group Discussion:

The leader reads aloud one suggestion at a time and asks that membe
them not identify themselves. Each recommendation is reviewed by the gro
are encouraged to say whether they agree and if they feel any of the suggest
tical.

The members decide if any of these suggestions should be submitted to
administrator. Part of the discussion should reflect the anticipated reactio
or administration, and how a possible compromise might be achieved. It is
members to explore whether this would be threatening in any way to them
ers.

This exercise is recommended with all group types. In those groups in e
development it may help members to explore their expectations. In groups
of development it might be an actual agent for change.

One possible outcome of this exercise is that group members come to fe
ble of finding ways to modify situations that affect their lives.

Creative Therapy II: 52 More Exercises for Groups

Exercise 52

THE PANIC BUTTON

Purpose:

1. To provide an opportunity for ventilating fears and anxiety.
2. To encourage empathy.
3. To enhance group identity and cohesion.

Materials:

One photocopy of the illustration for each group member; pens, pencils, crayons, or markers.

Description:

A. The leader begins the exercise by asking members to talk about what is commonly meant by a "panic button." Next, the leader encourages members to talk about how fears can be both real and imagined.
B. The materials are distributed, and the group leader asks how the illustration relates to the theme.
C. Members are told to draw in what makes them feel panicked, fearful, or anxious.

Group Discussion:

Members share their illustration and describe in detail what makes them panic. The rest of the group is encouraged to comment, and to offer suggestions about how to help cope with these fears.

Through this exercise, members can be directed toward expressing reassurance and support for one another. This may foster a sense of bonding and cohesion.

This exercise can be interpreted on many levels, and therefore is useful with a broad spectrum of groups.

Now there are **THREE** Volumes of *Creative Therapy*!

Please send me:

_____ Copies of *Creative Therapy: 52 Exercises for Groups*
_____ Copies of *Creative Therapy II: 52 More Exercises for Groups*
_____ Copies of *Creative Therapy III: 52 More Exercises for Groups*
(List Price: $21.95 each. Please add shipping noted below.*)

Shipping Charges
Up to $15.00 Order, Add $3.00 in US, $5.00 Foreign
$15 - $29.99 Order, Add $3.50 in US, $5.50 Foreign
$30 - $44.99 Order, Add $4.00 in US, $6.00 Foreign
$45 - $59.99 Order, Add $4.25 in US, $6.25 Foreign
Orders over $60, Add 7% in US, 10% Foreign
(Call for charges for 1, 2, or 3 day US delivery or Foreign air)

All orders from individuals and private institutions must be prepaid in full. Florida residents, add 7% sales tax. Prices and availability subject to change without notice.

For fastest service (purchase and credit card orders only)
CALL TOLL FREE 1-800-443-3364
Weekdays 9:00 - 5:00 Eastern Time
or
FAX 1-941-366-7971
24 hours a day

Check or money order enclosed (US funds only) $_____

Charge my (circle): Visa   MasterCard   American Express   Discover

Card # _____

Exp. Date _____ Daytime Phone # (_____)_____

Signature _____

Please fold on this line and the solid line below, tape (DO NOT STAPLE), and mail.

☐ Order enclosed (ship to name and address below).

☐ Please add my name to your mailing list and send me your latest catalog.
(If you ordered this copy from Professional Resource Exchange, your name is already on our Preferred-Customer Mailing List.)

Name _____
Address _____
Address _____
City/State/Zip _____

I am a _____ psychologist; _____ clinical social worker; _____ marriage & family therapist; _____mental health counselor; _____school psychologist; _____ psychiatrist; _____other: _____

THANK YOU!

Please fold on this line and the solid line above, tape (DO NOT STAPLE), and mail.

NO POSTAGE
NECESSARY
IF MAILED
IN THE
UNITED STATES

BUSINESS   REPLY   MAIL
FIRST-CLASS MAIL   PERMIT NO 445   SARASOTA FL

POSTAGE WILL BE PAID BY ADDRESSEE

PROFESSIONAL RESOURCE EXCHANGE INC
PO BOX 15560
SARASOTA FL 34277-9900